Dropshi

How to Build A Massive E-Commerce Business Using Shopify, Amazon FBA, Email Marketing and Facebook Advertising For A Passive Income and Financial Freedom

Written by

Nathan Michaud

Nathan Michaud

© Copyright 2019 by Nathan Michaud- All rights reserved

From a Declaration of Principles which was accepted and approved equally by a Committee of the American Bar Association and a Committee of Publishers and Associations. In no way is it legal to reproduce, duplicate, or transmit any part of this document in either electronic means or in printed format. Recording of this publication is strictly prohibited and any storage of this document is not allowed unless with written permission from the publisher.

The following book is produced with the goal of providing information that is as accurate and reliable as possible. Regardless, purchasing this book can be seen as consent to the fact that both the publisher and the author of this book are in no way experts on the topics discussed within and that any recommendations or suggestions that are made herein are for entertainment purposes only. Professionals should be consulted as needed prior to undertaking any of the action endorsed herein.

This declaration is deemed fair and valid by both the American Bar Association and the Committee of Publishers Association and is legally binding throughout the United States.

Financial Disclaimer:

I am not a financial advisor, this is not financial advice. This is not an investment guide nor investment advice. I am not recommending you buy any of the stocks listed here. Any form of investment or trading is liable to lose you money.

Furthermore, the transmission, duplication or reproduction of any of the following work including specific information will be considered an illegal act irrespective of if it is done electronically or in print. This extends to creating a secondary or tertiary copy of the work or a recorded copy and is only allowed with the express written consent from the Publisher. All additional right reserved.

The information in the following pages is broadly considered to be a truthful and accurate account of facts and as such any inattention, use or misuse of the information in question by the reader will render any resulting actions solely under their purview. There are no scenarios in which the publisher or the original author of this work can be in any fashion deemed liable for any hardship or damages that may befall them after undertaking information described herein.

Nathan Michaud

Additionally, the information in the following pages is intended only for informational purposes and should thus be thought of as universal. As befitting its nature, it is presented without assurance regarding its prolonged validity or interim quality. Trademarks that are mentioned are done without written consent and can in no way be considered an endorsement from the trademark holder.

Table of Contents

Preface 6

Chapter 1: High-Growth Businesses For Entrepreneurs 10

Chapter 2: Dropshipping in 2019 36

Chapter 3: Think Like An Entrepreneur 45

Chapter 4: Getting Started with Shopify 51

Chapter 5: Setting up Your First Shopify Dropshipping Store 56

Chapter 6: Finding Suppliers 76

Chapter 7: The Perfect Niche Research 83

Chapter 8: Pricing Strategy 93

Chapter 9: Legitimizing your Business 97

Chapter 10: Optimizing Your Dropshipping Website 102

Chapter 11: How to Develop Your Brand in 2019 110

Chapter 12: Email Marketing Strategies 117

Chapter 13: Facebook Advertising For Products in 2019 128

Chapter 14: Getting Started With FBA 148

Chapter 15: Affiliate Marketing and Other Income Streams 165

Chapter 16: Outsourcing For Dropshipping 176

Conclusion 180

Nathan Michaud

Preface

Being an online entrepreneur and making money online will give you the two most significant resources to raise my family – money, and freedom. That will change your life, and it will change the trajectory of your children's lives. Here is how you can do it and what you need to do to get there.

There is a global and collective frame of thinking that echoes in our mind. It says that wrapping ourselves in a suit and choking ourselves with a tie, sardined between commuters on the way to a job that doesn't pay enough and which has a boss who is ungrateful, along with colleagues who are ready to plunge the proverbial knife in the back, is the way to live our lives.

It also tells us that we should let our kids be raised by someone else, imparting their values and their attitudes on kids that will grow up mimicking them, at worst, or homogenizing them in the social environment that packed schools create. None of this is right, and none of this is healthy.

We do it because we are all caught up in a dream, much like Neo was in the classic Matrix movie. We are all caught up thinking that that lifestyle gives us the best stability and security to raise a family. It doesn't.

Many people, growing up, were told that they needed to work hard and get a good job. That is like a father telling the son to work hard, build his strength and muscles so he can get a job as a slave building the pyramid for the Pharaoh.

The prevailing wisdom in the last generation was that getting a job would ensure that you had food to eat and a roof over your head for the rest of your life. But that's not true, is it? How many people do you know who have lost their jobs when the company was not making a profit? How many people do you know who are living in excessive debt while they work two, or even three jobs? Are you doing the same?

Don't fool yourself. If you are working a job for someone, it doesn't matter who that is, whether it is a Fortune 500 company or a mom and pop business on Main Street, you are still a slave, and your job is not secure. The moment they have no use for you, you are back on the unemployment line.

If you are working for someone, just make sure it is a temporary gig while you save up enough to get your own laptop because that laptop is your salvation. It is your ticket to freedom, and most importantly it is your ticket to wealth and advancement. But there is one more thing—even if you don't want to be rich and powerful, you should still want your freedom.

It is also not always about working in some corporate office in a major metropolitan city, it could be just the opposite, you may want to pursue a life of spirituality and Zen. The attitude and state of mind that one has to maintain just so he/she could support his family with a corporate job may distract from those spiritual aspirations.

Both kinds of people seem to turn to the Internet, and this started as early as the late 90s and early 00s. After bouncing around in the midst of figuring out what would work, many internet entrepreneurs eventually came across blogging and writing for hire.

Armed with just a simple laptop, early entrepreneurs started freelancing as writers for other blog site owners and soon developed their own blog. From there, they jumped to writing books and ghostwriting for publishers. Within a couple of years as the indie publishing industry took off, many started publishing their own books.

The money they made was modest but enough to keep them on their feet. When they worked, they got paid. When self-publishing started to catch on, many writers started to notice a new revenue stream – this is what we call Passive Income these days. It's the work that you did once, but kept getting recurring income from it, sometimes even years later.

Online businesses have given these people the freedom to do all that they thought was possible. They get to spend time with their family and raise them without needing strangers to raise their kids. Instead of allowing their children to be part of the herd, they had the time to guide them.

Researchers have found that the biggest thing holding people back is their mindset. That's what you have to relinquish. You can do this and there are tools that will help you do it.

Reclaim your freedom and you will be able to turn your life around. One more thing – Your lifestyle will be free. You will get to travel, your family will get to travel to some of the world's most beautiful places and soaked it all in. You will still work and be with yet see the world.

Chapter 1: High-Growth Businesses For Entrepreneurs in 2019

There are a number of other business that you can undertake once you start becoming familiar with the online world. Aside from audiobooks that are exploding at the moment (don't forget to get the free guide to starting your audiobook business), you can look at the following five areas:

1. **Drop-shipping**
2. **Informational products**
3. **Affiliate marketing**
4. **White labeling**
5. **Self-publishing**

Either you can build a business around one of these areas, or you can start with self-publishing and then tackle each business in turn over time as you get more cash flow.

So let's say you do the audiobooks first. You can then branch into informational products, then roll that into affiliate marketing, then roll that into drop-shipping, and then expand that into white labeling.

Let's start with informational products. This is as simple as it sounds. Anything that provides information, things like product reviews, or how to use certain products, is an informational product. If you are, let's say, a pilot working for an airline, you can create information about how to fly a plane, or how to read a chart, or how to land in bad weather.

Dropshipping is a business model of supply chain management where retailers don't have to maintain or manage their inventory. They can promote the products of their suppliers and earn a handsome commission for doing so. A dropshipper is essentially an intermediary between suppliers and customers. The dropshipper will transfer the order information to the supplier while holding onto a certain portion of the payment received, as commission and the supplier will directly dispatch the product from the warehouse to the customer.

These are all informational products. That is one way of approaching it. The second way of approaching it is from the opposite end. You scour the internet and look for what kinds of information people are looking for, and then you find a writer to write about that. You can get as granular as you like or you can be as general as you like. In time you will get a feel for what sells

The next is affiliate marketing. This is where you use

content—like informational products, blogs, personal stories, anything that you can think of that will interest someone—and you put them online for anyone to read for free. Then you place links in them to various products. So, for instance, if you're writing about pilot stuff, then you can add links for aircraft models or flight simulation software. That link will then take them to Amazon or some other vendor, and when they make a purchase, you will get a small commission.

As you can tell, the key to this is volume. So, you want to generate as much interest from your informational products so that readers will click on your links. Say, for instance, one out of ten people who click the link make the purchase, and one out of ten readers click the link; so that means that out of 100 people reading your article, ten people will click the link and one person will make a purchase.

Let's say you make a $1 from that purchase. That means that if you get 10,000 people to read your article, you will make $100. Now let's say that for every ten Twitter followers who receive your tweet, one person visits your article. To get 10,000 readers, you need 100,000 Twitter followers. Do you see how this works?

Build your following, and the sales will roll in, regardless of what you have to sell. That is the nature of the online world and how you make anything into a high-growth business.

The next item on the list is drop-shipping. Drop-shipping is amazing once you have built your viewership and online followers. You create a store that specializes in a certain kind of product. This will allow you to focus your online content and informational products to focus on niches—like the flying example discussed earlier. You can then create a store that sells all kinds of flight stuff and have it drop-shipped. Drop-shipment means that the maker, or stockist, of the product does not send you the product but ships it directly to your buyer once they have made a sale with you.

One of the best places to do this is Alibaba.com. You create relationships with manufacturers, and whenever you send them an order, they put your name on the packaging and send it directly to your customer. How great is that? Now imagine you have already been in self-publishing or informational products for a year and you have a million customers following you or reading your blogs, website, and tweets and you have products that you are selling. In addition to the audiobooks that they have, they will also buy related stuff. That is a great way to monetize your followers.

That then leads to white labeling, where you can create your own brand of almost anything. You can even create your own brand of makeup. Get a white label manufacturer that you trust to slap your name on the packaging and sell that as your own.

In the dropshipping model of business, the parties involved include the supplier, a dropshipping store, and the customers. The customers will order the product from the dropshipping store. The store will then transfer the details of the order to the supplier along with customer information. The supplier will then directly ship the product to the customer. The dropshipping store will always sell the product at a higher price than the cost of acquisition and that's their profit margin. For instance, if the wholesale rate of a product is $150, then the dropshipping store can sell the same product for $200 and so the profit that you make as a dropshipper is $50!

As a dropshipper, there are a couple of aspects of the business that you need to understand. You have the power to decide the price of the products. If you want to start wholesaling your product, then you can do so without partnering with other manufacturers by using services like AliExpress, eBay, Amazon, or even Shopify. The final aspect of the business that you need to understand is that you will earn through arbitrage.

Why Dropshipping

Well, dropshipping is certainly a lucrative business model, but here is a list of the different benefits it offers that make dropshipping more appealing.

Easy to Enter

As a dropshipper, you don't have to pay upfront for the inventory. You only need to pay fees for hosting and your domain. Since there is no inventory, loss of revenue is highly unlikely. You have the option of upselling your products.

Convenience

Dropshipping is quite convenient for the dropshipper as well as the supplier. The dropshipper doesn't have to worry about shipping or packaging the product. The supplier doesn't have to worry about marketing and other promotional activities. As a dropshipper, you also have the option of working with various wholesalers simultaneously.

Scale and Remodel

Since your business model is fully digitized, you don't need to worry about storage facilities, and it makes dropshipping an easy business model to scale. Even if one product doesn't sell well on your dropshipping store, you have the option of moving onto better products.

Less Risk

It is quite inexpensive to start a dropshipping store. All that you need is a domain and a hosting service, and you can get started immediately. The risk involved in this form of business is quite low.

Dropshipping is a lucrative business model, especially with the different benefits it offers. It doesn't mean that there aren't any drawbacks for this business model. If you want to start a business, it is important that you are aware of the benefits as well as the drawbacks it must optimize your business. Here are a couple of drawbacks of the dropshipping model.

High Competition

Competition is prevalent in all walks of life and e-commerce stores are no exception. As a store owner, you must strive to stand out from the crowd by providing high-quality and unique products to your customers. High competition proves that the niche you selected is profitable, but it can be a thorn in your side if you aren't careful. New stores keep popping up almost every day and you need to make your store stand out from those of your competitors.

Low Margins

Dropshipping isn't a short-term business idea. If you want to be a successful dropshipper, then you must be in it for the long run. It is all about staying in the game and steadily making your way up the ladder. You must come up with a method to increase your profit margin. Instead of selling ten units per day, try to sell about 50 or so to increase your profits. A great thing about dropshipping is that you don't have to worry about logistics, so you can work on scaling your business.

Full Liability

As a dropshipper, it is quite probable that you might end up selling a product that you have never seen. Therefore, the chances of the product not living up to the consumer's expectations can be quite high. If the customer is not satisfied with the product, then the liability rests on you to process the refund and return the product to the supplier, so you must take some time and create a perfectly understandable and unambiguous return policy for your business.

Managing Orders

One aspect of the business that most fledgling dropshippers struggle with is when the demand for their product increases rapidly. You need to manage all the orders that fly in and you must not let it overwhelm you.

Shopify

Now that you know what dropshipping is about, the next step is to learn about Shopify. In this book, you will learn about setting up a dropshipping business with Shopify. Before you learn about starting your business, you must understand the platform that you are going to use.

Shopify is a cloud-based shopping cart option. For a monthly fee, it gives you access to an administrative panel that lets you store data, add products, and process the orders you receive. It also offers several free and paid-for design templates for your online store. The themes available are quite clean and modern. Also, Shopify offers different editing tools that you can use to create a theme that suits your brand well. When you subscribe to Shopify, it also offers secure and reliable hosting for your dropshipping website. You don't have to worry about any technical issues like the site crashing or getting hacked.

Also, Shopify provides great 24/7-customer support. Whenever you find yourself in trouble or anything like that, you can immediately contact the customer support. For a dropshipper, Shopify is the perfect option for everything they need.

Pros and Cons

Easy to Use
Shopify is quite easy to use, and you don't have to be tech-savvy to use this platform. It is quite simple to add products and process bulk orders. The web design is user-friendly, and the editing tools are simple to use.

Cost-Effective
The startup cost on Shopify is quite low and the monthly fees payable are certainly affordable. The basic plan costs about $29 per month and the mid-level plan will cost you $79 per month. You must select a plan that meets your needs.

Themes

As a merchant on Shopify, you can choose from a vast array of themes that are free and are adapted for mobile use. There are free and paid-for options to choose from.

Shopify is the go-to destination for a lot of dropshippers because of its integration with Ordoro and Oberlo.

Support

The technical support team on Shopify is available at any time and you can reach them through your phone, live chat, or even email. There are various self-help options available as well. There are no business hours applicable for the customer support team and they are available 24/7.

There has been a significant increase in the client load on Shopify and their support team is finding it difficult to keep up with this increased demand. The customer support service might not always be as quick as you hope for.

Functionality

There are various pre-set features that a merchant will need while setting up a store on Shopify; however, there will be times when a business might have a specific requirement and Shopify might not have the necessary features to accommodate those needs. This problem can be easily fixed if you purchase some add-ons. The add-ons certainly make your life easier, but they aren't free and are expensive. This can increase your monthly fees payable.

Transaction Fee

Most online shopping carts have reduced their shopping fees, but according to the pricing plan you opt for, you will need to pay a 0.2 to 0.5% as transaction fees on Shopify.

Email Marketing

Once you set up a store on Shopify, your work doesn't end. In fact, as the owner of an e-commerce store, your work has only just begun. You need to work on marketing and promoting your business. One of the best ways in which you can market your online business is through email marketing. It is the best channel that you can employ to engage in a one-on-one conversations with your existing and potential customers.

Especially in a business like dropshipping, it is important that you not just acquire, but also retain your customers. Why do you need email marketing for your dropshipping business?

Targeted Marketing

With email marketing, you have the option to target specific segments of the customer market. You will initially work with fewer products during the initial phase of your dropshipping business. If you have fewer products to work with, then you need to make sure that you target a specific audience. For instance, if you notice that some customers add products to their cart but don't make a purchase on your website, then you need to target such customers in your subsequent email marketing campaign. You can target such customers by offering them a discount or any other attractive offer to compel them to make a purchase. You can design a specific email marketing campaign to target all those customers who have made a purchase and encourage them to become repeat customers.

Measurable and Data-Driven

Knowledge is power when it comes to email marketing. There are various metrics that you can obtain from your email marketing campaign to design your other marketing strategies. For instance, you can obtain metrics like the click-through rate, open rate, opt-out rate, and so on. These different parameters will help you organize or reorganize your marketing efforts to optimize your marketing campaigns.

Traffic and Sales

Sales are the primary priority for any e-commerce business owner. In a dropshipping business, you must work on increasing the traffic to your site if you want to increase your sales. The best way to do this is by mailing your product catalog to your target audience. If you implement email marketing properly, you can derive exceptional results and increase your sales.

Affordable

Email marketing is perhaps the most affordable method of marketing these days. Apart from the initial start-up and implementation costs, there is hardly any other maintenance cost involved with this method of marketing. You can reach a huge audience quite easily and it will not burn a hole in your pocket. For instance, if you use MailChimp, you can send about 12,000 emails every month for free! So, you need to select a business plan and an email service that will suit your needs.

Omnipresent

Almost everyone has at least one email address these days. Most e-commerce businesses require an email address of the user for signing up and this coupled with the exponential rise in the popularity of online shopping, all online shoppers have at least one email address, so it is safe to say that emails are an omnipresent form of communication. You will learn about the different email marketing strategies that you can employ to grow your email list and successfully sell to your list in the coming chapters.

Google AdWords

In 2016, Google AdWords generated revenue of over $70 billion. This metric certainly shows that a lot of people are using Google AdWords because it is quite effective. Google AdWords is an online advertising platform that helps advertisers display ads, product listings, video content, and the like for a fee.

AdWords is an advertising service that businesses can use to display their ads on Google and its related advertising network. AdWords is a program that lets the businesses set a budget for advertising and you only need to pay when your target audience views the ad. The primary focus of this service is on keywords. If you use AdWords, then you can create relevant ads by using the keywords that people usually use to search for your business, niche, or industry on Google. Whenever the user types in the relevant keyword, then your ad will be shown next to the search results. The ads are usually shown under the heading "Sponsored Links" on the Google results.

Here are the different reasons why you must include Google AdWords in your marketing strategy.

No Minimum Investment

If you have a limited budget or are just getting started with online marketing, then you must include Google AdWords. In fact, it isn't just small businesses that use this service, but even the large and well-established businesses as well. Even if you have a huge marketing budget, it always makes sense to play it a little safe, at least initially, before you decide to try newer channels. With this option, there is no minimum investment you need to make or fix a monthly advertising budget. It means that the risk involved in this form of advertising is low compared to other options that require an upfront payment. Some keywords do cost more than the others, but if you use the keywords wisely, you can make a dent in the market.

Results

This ad service is affordable, and you need to pay only when you get the results. It is similar to a pay-per-click advertisement wherein you will have to pay only when someone clicks on the specific link. If you set up your advertising campaign properly and incorporate the relevant and negative keywords, then the clicks that you pay for will mostly be for good future prospects and potential clients for your business. You can also use AdWords for retargeting all those users who might have clicked on your ad in the past but aren't your customers yet, it is a great way to generate leads for your dropshipping business.

Good Timing

Whenever someone searches for something in Google, it is quite likely that they are looking for something specific in that moment. Google AdWords gives the business the perfect opportunity to market to their future prospects at the moment when they are considering a buying decision or are thinking about making a purchase. Before the advent of digital marketing and advertising, businesses used to list their services in telephone directories under a category that is similar to or related to their business. Think of Google AdWords as the modern-day telephone directory or register.

Placement

It isn't just timing that matters, but even the locality matters as well. If your ads are being shown to those customers who live beyond the places that you can deliver to, then it doesn't make any sense to invest in such advertisements. Google AdWords also helps with geographical targeting.

Engaging the Customers

When it comes to content marketing, videos are the most effective means of doing this. Research shows that a significant percentage of users are likely to buy a product after they watch an online ad for it. Did you know that Google AdWords manages YouTube advertising as well? It means that if you use Google AdWords, you have an opportunity to get your ads on YouTube videos that are related to your business or products.

SEO

Search Engine Optimization or SEO is quite important if you want to generate traffic to your website or you want to increase the online visibility of your online business. When you start using important keywords for your AdWords campaign, then the same keywords can be used in your SEO strategy as well to improve the online visibility of your website.

Nathan Michaud
Affiliate Marketing

Affiliate marketing is a phrase that you might have stumbled across online. There are tens of thousands of articles telling you why you must be minting money with affiliate marketing, and you might feel a little left out if your bank account isn't clocking up cash while you are sleeping. What exactly is affiliate marketing and how can you make use of it for generating a steady stream of passive income for yourself? To put it simply, affiliate marketing is the process of promoting or selling someone else's product or service. You earn a commission on any of the sales made or click-through to a given affiliate site. Doesn't that sound quite simple? In theory, you can have a website without any products or services of your own. It can be a blog, an online journal, or anything similar to it. As long as there is some relation with the product or the service, you are set. Maintaining a website costs money and with affiliate marketing, you can cover all those costs and earn more money. It doesn't cost the owner anything to sign up for an affiliate program and the business owner doesn't have to pay anything until he makes a sale, so it is a win-win situation for both the parties involved.

In this book, you will learn about affiliate marketing, the benefits it offers, about selecting an affiliate program, and the different strategies that you can use to generate income from affiliate marketing.

Selling a product can be difficult, even more so when you aren't able to reach out to your target audience. You might at times need to opt for other means of selling your product. On the other hand, you might need some extra money. In cases like these, both the parties can use affiliate marketing. In simple terms, in affiliate marketing, the vendor can sell their products or services by making use of an affiliate. The affiliate will be responsible for marketing the products to potential customers, allowing the vendor to make a sale, and in turn, the vendor will pay the affiliate for all the effort that they have put in to make that sale. The founder of PC Flowers & Gifts, William J. Tobin, is responsible for creating the concept of affiliate marketing. They made use of Prodigy network for increasing their sales and in turn paid Prodigy Network for the services they offered. You might not have realized it yet, but affiliate marketing is quite prevalent. The simplest form of affiliate marketing can be writing a review of products or services posted on any form of media and the Internet. Making use of the Internet for affiliate marketing has become an increasingly popular practice these days. Companies like Amazon have managed to create their own affiliate program and it has been developing since it was launched in 1996. It is a common practice these days and it is an easy way to earn money, when done properly.

Strategies to Use

Here are a couple of strategies that you can make use of.

A YouTube channel or a Blog Reviewing Products

Blogs provide their readers with useful reviews, articles, and product reviews. Whenever a potential client searches for a product or service he or she is interested in, they can find the reviews on your blog, purchase the product or service by following the affiliate link on your blog, and you will be paid a commission for the sale. It is not easy to create an audience base and it takes considerable time and effort to create a blog that others will want to follow. You can improve your visibility in search engine rankings by creating a YouTube account and by posting videos pertaining to product reviews. You can post the affiliate links to the products you reviewed in the description box.

Promotion and review on your YouTube video or blog

You can make money through affiliate marketing by promoting or reviewing products or services on YouTube or blog. Reviewing products or services is easier than to create new blog posts from scratch. Each blog posts created builds the authority of your blog in the search engine and drives more traffic to your blog. Sharing a product, event program, or seminar can also be promoted on your blog or YouTube channel.

Promoting Products and Services to your Email Listing.

When visitors visit your blog and read your blog articles, a lot of them will end up clicking the affiliate links of products or services you recommend on your blog, which will earn you money. If there is a product or service that you want to share with your followers, sending out an e-mail regarding the recommendation is the best option; however, in promoting products to your email listing, keep in mind these two important rules to follow:

Never recommend or promote a product you have not used personally or feel comfortable using. Think about your followers and if you want them to stay loyal to you, then you must think of their needs as well. Maintain equilibrium between quality and value. Don't bombard your followers with a lot of emails. After all, you don't want to start spamming them, do you? You must be able to provide your customers with content that provides some value to them.

Benefits of Affiliate Marketing

Affiliate marketing not only complements but is also being used as a replacement for the more conventional marketing strategies these days. In affiliate marketing, you don't have to spend time, effort, or finances on creating a new product or service. You simply have to provide a platform that other vendors can make use of for selling their products and services. Let us take a look at all the different benefits that affiliate marketing offers.

Endless Possibilities

One of the easiest ways to start your home-based company is to take up affiliate marketing. As such, there is no limit on the income that you can earn from affiliate marketing. Also, affiliate marketing is considered a low-risk business model.

It is convenient

With affiliate marketing, you have the option of working at your convenience. You are your boss and are therefore in charge of your working hours. When you work for someone else, you are always bound by their rules. There might be times when you need to push your working hours to meet a deadline. With affiliate marketing, you can forget about all this and set your working hours according to your needs and your lifestyle.

You can Track Your Progress

It is quite easy to track the metrics to check your progress with affiliate marketing. You can track the number of people who you are reaching out to, the products that you sold directly or indirectly, and also the profits you are raking in.

Autonomy to Select the Products and Projects

You have complete autonomy to select the products or

projects you want to be an affiliate marketer for. You can opt for those products that interest you. You don't have to take up things that you aren't passionate about and can do something that you enjoy.

Work from Anywhere

As an affiliate marketer, you will not have a fixed workplace or working hours. You can pretty much work from anywhere in the world as long as you have a laptop and a reliable Internet connection. You can work according to your convenience and can instead focus on doing the things that you enjoy.

Steady Cash Flow

One of the prominent advantages of becoming an affiliate marketer is that it helps you generate a steady cash flow. You will certainly receive a paycheck even if you work for someone, but you will need to follow the rules and regulations that your employer sets. With affiliate marketing, you are your boss and can work according to your convenience and still earn a steady income. You can also retain your regular job and use affiliate marketing to generate some additional income for yourself.

Facebook Ads

Social media is an integral part of the marketing campaigns for most businesses these days. It is a great way to build an audience, increase engagement, and share content. If you don't want to miss out on reaching a large audience, then you need to use Facebook ads. Facebook is amongst the most popular social media platforms these days and it is a great place for marketing. Here are the different reasons why you must use Facebook ads in your marketing campaign.

Affordable

You can decide your advertising budget on Facebook. Not just that, you can also set when you want Facebook to start and stop showing the ads. The higher your budget, the greater your reach. In fact, Facebook ads have a great ROI and it is one thing that all marketers will unanimously agree upon. It works well for B2B as well as B2C companies.

Audience

On average, people tend to spend about 40 minutes on Facebook. Apart from that, more than 2 billion people have Facebook accounts and about 1.55 billion users access the platform every month, so it is quite safe to say that most of your target audience is active on Facebook.

Target Users

Facebook provides a lot of information about the people active on this platform. Facebook ads help you target audiences who are most likely to engage with your brand or business. This platform allows you to target your audience according to different criteria like their age, gender, location, job profile, usual behavior, interests, and various other parameters. You also have the option of targeting lookalike audiences on Facebook. It means that you can specifically target those users who are quite similar to your existing audience.

Retargeting

You don't just specifically target a certain audience, but you also have the option of retargeting your audience. It means that you can target all those people who have visited your website in the past, have used your app, or have shared their email address with you. It is quite likely that those who are familiar with your business will be repeat customers.

Easy to use

It is quite easy to set up an advertising campaign on Facebook. You need to select the type of ad you want to run, define your target audience, select a budget and set your timeframe. Facebook ads offer a high degree of customizability and there are multiple formats to choose from. You not only have the option of choosing a pay-per-click model, but you can also opt for a pay per impression, like or action campaigns as well. You will learn more about setting up and running a successful ad campaign on Facebook in the coming chapters.

Analytics

Advertising on Facebook provides you the opportunity to reach various users regardless of whether they are in a buying frame of mind or not. It is not a limitation, but an effective opportunity to gather data. Your ads might not be effective for closing a sale, but they will certainly help increase awareness for your business and capture leads. Facebook provides a lot of information that you can use to analyze your marketing campaign and make it more effective. You can use different metrics like reach, frequency, likes, or impressions you receive to calculate the ROI of your ads. These real-time metrics come in handy if you want to increase the efficiency and the effectiveness of your marketing campaign.

Custom Button

Most digital ads come with a call-to-action button that leads the viewer to a landing page. It is quite effective because it helps the user gather more information about a specific product before they make a decision. If you use Facebook ads, you have the option to customize the call-to-action button to include different actions that are beneficial for your e-commerce website like "contact us, apply now, purchase now," and so on.

Video ads

We live in a world where the rules of advertising and marketing are undergoing a massive overhaul. Video ads are the latest trend in the field of marketing and it is here to stay. Facebook allows you to create video ads that help grab the attention of the viewer.

If you want to increase the reach of your brand on social media, then Facebook is your go-to option. Facebook ads help increase the awareness of your business, attract and nurture leads, and help convert existing users into loyal customers!

Chapter 2: Dropshipping vs Other Income Streams

All the businesses you will be looking at to make your laptop lifestyle a reality are not limited to physical or downloadable products. Ideally, you should have your finger in all the pies that you can. There are products and electronic downloads that you can deal with, as well have online assets that distribute content.

The entire online universe can be divided into two types of product. The first kind is the physical product – and you can think of this as anything that needs to get shipped to you. The second thing is anything that you can download – images, movies, books, and so on.

These two broad categories can then be divided further into the five top business areas that will yield you the most bang for your effort.

The five business areas are as follows:

1. Self- Publishing
2. Drop Shipping
3. Affiliate Marketing

4. Content Creation

5. Fulfilled By amazon

So, to reiterate, self-publishing includes E-books, print on demand books, audiobooks, and anything that you can create and set up for download sales. You can typically leverage online repositories like Kindle by Amazon to upload your books, Audibly by Amazon to upload your audiobooks, Artpal to upload your paintings, and Udemy to upload online courses and the list goes on. You can even make animated movies and upload them on YouTube.

Affiliate marketing is where you typically neither own the product nor stock it, but you act as a conduit to facilitate sales. You don't even need to have a sales page. What you do is have an interesting page, something like websites and informational content, and blogs. They primarily involve the creation of content that can be consumed remotely, i.e. things that can be downloaded. Typical models of this kind of opportunity are to create free content that relates to skill, knowledge or instruction. An example of this would be websites that teach a particular set of skills like sewing, or even life experiences. The content on those sites are free, but there are related links to products that may be of interest to people who are interested in the information the site provided so, if it is a sewing site, then there could be links to sewing products. Every time a visitor to the site clicks on that link and a sale is completed, you receive a commission.

The third on the list is content creation. Content creation can be a revenue generator of its own, and you don't have to add affiliate links to it; instead, you outsource the ad generation responsibilities to a third party like Google. Google sells advertisements to a wide variety of people and they will automatically place ads on your page depending on the visitor. Not every visitor sees the same advertisement. If you go to your favorite site, you may see an advertisement for electronics but, if your spouse goes to the same site on their device, they may see an advertisement more related to them like art supplies. Google tailors the advertisement to the visitor, and that increases the chances of a click. You just have to focus on having good content. Fulfilled By is a term that is recent in the online world. It was created by Amazon, but Amazon is not the only place where you can use this format of selling to customers. Let's back up for a second to make the explanation a little meaningful. The biggest problem in online product marketing is that individual sellers do not have the track record and credibility that will motivate a customer to go through with a purchase. Someone visiting Amazon is more likely to make a purchase than that same person visiting flybynight.com for the same product.

On top of that, if you are a serious seller, you need an online presence with all the complications that come with it and more so, you need warehousing facilities to ship all these products. The headaches do not end there. You also need to be able to ship cost effectively. When you join the Amazon program (called FBA – Fulfilled By Amazon) all you have to do is ship your inventory to Amazon, they will warehouse all of it and then you will promote your product on their website and anywhere else you would like to promote it (including via your own content, YouTube, Google ads – in any way that you can think of). Once the sale is made, you get the price that you set minus a cut for Amazon.

The next on the list is drop shipping and this involves all kinds of goods that can be sourced anywhere in the world and shipped to your customer. It typically works out on a specialty web storefront, or an online mall, where you source products from sellers who are willing to send the product directly to your customer.

Your customer pays you upon making the order, you then take that order and make a purchase from your vendor and get them to send the product directly to your customer. You will have to front the payment to your vendor.

Finally, there is also something called white labeling. This is even more involved, but, nonetheless, can be a fairly significant profit potential. This will not be discussed in this book because the return on effort is not as great as the other areas of business that readily lend itself to profitable laptop lifestyles.

White labeling happens when not only does the vendor ship the product to your customer, but the label on the product carries your brand, so the customer sees the product as yours and not someone else's. Just keep this in the back of your mind.

You will see that there is a core distinction between the five areas and, at the same time, there are close similarities. Each is a million dollar business on its own, and each has common core competencies that are identical to some degree. This means that you can specialize in those core areas and outsource a lot of the other work so that you can build a highly profitable business that has all the components, reaping large profits while you sip drinks served in coconuts and watch the tide roll in.

Out of the five areas that you could invest your time and effort in, there are two that are going to be major avenues of profit in the coming year. The key success factor in a laptop lifestyle is that you put in the least amount of repetitive effort for the most amount of recurring return. That way, once you stop focusing on one area and you shift that focus on to the next, the first area you focused on is still generating income, while you avert your attention to the second area. By the time you get to the third, the first and second endeavors are still generating income and this keeps going.

When looking at self-publishing, the king of the hill is Amazon. Under the Amazon umbrella, there are a number of self-publishing avenues. The oldest is the Kindle E-book platform where you can write books of fiction or non-fiction and put it on their website for free. There are a long string of millionaires who have been writing books for this channel for more than a decade now, and then they have books that are printed on demand. Admittedly, the growth for this market is shrinking, as the millennial reading market prefers to consume their content in electronic form or in Audiobook form.

This brings us to the important part of this chapter and the area that you should focus on right now. Even if you don't decide to give up your day job and become an online maverick, this is one area that you definitely should jump into with both feet without delay.

This is the area of audiobooks. Audiobooks have opened up a whole new market among Millennials and the prior generations alike. The appeal of audiobooks is that one can get the benefit of reading, while not having to read. It stimulates the imagination and, more importantly, it has been, as an industry, one of the fastest growing in the last year and is expected to be the fastest growing segment of the self-publishing eco-system.

If you have already been publishing books, then this is just a stone's throw in terms of a reach for you because you already have the rights to your material – you now just need to convert it to audio format. If you have a great voice and are good at reading, there are numerous free applications that you can download on your computer and get started. However, it is recommended that you outsource this to a professional.

Outsourcing avenues will be discussed in the last chapter. For now, let's just focus on audiobooks.

Audiobooks come under self-publishing and have a large margin potential. They also have volume potential and a good chance that there will be significant residual income – or what is called in this book, 'passive income.' Your effort to convert the book happens once, then the book just needs a little promoting and it will keep generating sales based on word of mouth, social interest, and the feedback that a good quality book or audiobook will receive.

Numerous early-starters have had a lot of success with audiobooks, mostly by making a lot of mistakes in the process of getting up to speed and penetrating the market. You can shortcut some of these mistakes by doing your homework. The other area that this chapter is about is drop shipping. If self-publishing is not your thing, then maybe drop shipping will tickle your fancy.

Drop shipping allows you to scale up to whatever you can afford, and to do it slowly without the need for warehousing. That drives your overheads and financial costs so that you can focus on advertising and content creation around your niche. For example, a hobby site that you can get quad copter parts from, has a really powerful blog that has taught many people a huge amount about quads and the racing aspect of it. Every time there is a notification that their blog has been updated, people are ready to jump in and read what they have to say. It turns out that, for most people that read the blog, every time that they have something new, it is probably bought.

The drop shipping aspect of it is interesting too. Most drop shipped products are also based on content that is on YouTube, and how-to articles that then lead to the store. It takes too much time to write multiple articles every week, so it is outsourced to freelance writers. That has resulted in strong traffic from both areas that should also be sought to develop – contemporaneous visitors who do Google searches and find the content, or from subscribers who visit as soon as they receive a notification that there is new content waiting. With those two avenues of visitors, the click-through rate will be fairly consistent. Pro tip: On the checkout thank you page, monetize that with Google ads.

Usually, those ads show the visitor what they are interested in, and that takes them to another site and, since they are already in the buying mood with their credit card out, they make more purchases. Niche products get sold, and you get Google revenue because of the content.

That brings us to the next chapter on content development.

Chapter 3: Think Like An Entrepreneur

One thing that we want to stress to you is that when you choose to run a dropshipping site, you are taking on a serious job. If you treat your dropshipping work like it is nothing more than a hobby, something fun to do on the weekends, then you will never succeed, and you will most likely struggle to find good suppliers. If you want to become successful in this endeavor, you must learn to think like an entrepreneur.

What is an entrepreneur? An entrepreneur is a creator, they are a manager, and most importantly, they are a force that can change the world. They build businesses as a lifestyle. They don't focus on one sole business for the rest of their life; instead, they place their attention on building a business up until it is profitable, then either sell it or automate it before moving onto another endeavor. While you might want to focus solely on dropshipping for your e-commerce career, there is a lot that you can learn from how entrepreneurs operate. This chapter is all about helping you learn how to think like an entrepreneur. Here are a series of rules that most entrepreneurs follow. When you adopt these rules and hold them tightly, you will be setting yourself up for success when it comes to running your business. Anyone can set up a dropshipping website, but it takes the heart of an entrepreneur to be able to run one successfully.

Entrepreneur Rule 1: Focus on the bottom line

Any entrepreneur worth his salt will tell you that the whole point of running a business is to make a profit. Money is the lifeblood of any professional organization, including your dropshipping website. The more money that you earn, the more you can invest into expanding your operation. This pursuit of money should shape your decision-making process when it comes to making strategies for your business. The first question you should always ask when evaluating an aspect of your business is: how is this helping me make money?

There will always be plenty of "good ideas" that exist in the marketplace. And since you're just starting out, you will have the opportunity to think of plenty of ideas that seem good but don't lead you towards making a profit. Before you commit to any plan, you should have the ability to clearly explain to others how this is going to increase your bottom line. If you can't figure out where the money is coming from or if the investment seems to be too costly, go back to the drawing board.

In addition to planning accordingly, you must also be willing to kill ideas that clearly aren't working. While it is important to be patient in the world of online business, sometimes an idea ends up costing you too much money and brings little results. There can be a strong urge to believe that "eventually it will pay off," but if you hold onto a failing strategy for too long, it could do a lot more damage than you think.

Experimentation is an important part of dropshipping; looking for the right niche is always a bit of a gamble, and sometimes you can get burned. This is part of the process. However, if you aren't focused on the bottom line, you might make the mistake of staying in the niche for too long. Once it's clear that you aren't getting enough sales or that no one is showing any interest, it's time to move on. While it sucks that you invested time, energy and maybe even money into this niche, it isn't the end of the world. You've learned valuable data about your customer. An entrepreneur focused on being profitable will cut his losses early and be better off for it.

Entrepreneur Rule 2: Be willing to take risks

Entrepreneurship and e-commerce is all about risk and reward. You can't get to great rewards without taking risks. While it is true that sometimes a risk can be foolish, such as betting your life savings on the ponies, that doesn't mean that all risk is bad. An entrepreneur is not only willing to take risks but also willing to do the legwork to ensure that the risk they are taking will get them somewhere successful. We don't know everything, and we certainly don't know the future. There will always be a margin for error, but you are not defined by the times that your risks end up failing. You are defined by your successes. However, you cannot become successful without risking failure.

The biggest failure of all is the fear of moving forward because you don't want to suffer from the risks. But in the end, you have a chance to achieve the goals that you have set for yourself. If you always hold back or refuse to invest due to fear of risk, then you won't be successful. Of course, this isn't to say that you should act recklessly. Instead, focus on trying to mitigate risk as much as possible, while at the same time accepting that risks are inherent in the world of commerce. The goal is to have more wins than losses, but losses aren't nearly as bad as simply standing still.

Entrepreneur Rule 3: Make a work schedule and then stick to it

If you desire to run a successful dropshipping organization, then you're going to need to craft a plan for how you want to work week to week. If you are doing this full time, then you are going to want to have specific hours planned out to spend in the office each day. Set a schedule, and then hold yourself to it. If you work another job, then you'll definitely need to create a schedule that will allow you to have the necessary time to work on your dropshipping business.

Creating a schedule and then sticking to it is a discipline. However, it is the singular thing that will define whether you are successful or not in just about any endeavor. No one is going to run your business for you, unless you are willing to hire them. Even then, it's still your responsibility to watch over them and make sure your employee is doing a good job. Ultimately, the ability to sit down and focus, day after day, is what will push your company over the top. A schedule will give you the space and time necessary to work on your business. Without a schedule, you will likely work in sporadic bursts. This is a terrible way to operate a company.

Imagine if your favorite store worked like that. Imagine how it would operate if it was randomly open for a brief period of time. No one would know when to show up, and eventually, they would lose interest in the company. Stability is the major factor in just about any kind of entrepreneurial success. This takes hard work, and it requires a willingness to make sacrifices, but when you adhere to a schedule, you are setting yourself up for the highest success.

Chapter 4: Getting Started with Shopify

If you are looking to sell products online, whether through dropshipping or just selling things that you produce on a large scale for your business, then Shopify is definitely one of the tools that you should consider using. It is a large-scale web sales platform that allows you to have your own website geared entirely towards the purpose of selling products.

This means that Shopify can help you organize your products in a neat and efficient manner. With hundreds of apps available, both free and paid, you can set up your own storefront that will provide everything that a business needs.

Signing up for Shopify is easy as well. They offer several different tiers of membership; each tier provides different benefits depending on what you are looking for. They charge a monthly fee but don't charge transaction fees. If you're interested in trying out Shopify but aren't sure if you want to commit to paying for it, they do offer a free trial that will let you test it out.

After you have successfully signed up for Shopify, you'll be able to build your own website using Shopify's themes and then customize its look, colors, and the content inside. Shopify will take you through everything step by step, helping you create the perfect digital storefront for your online business.

Shopify has an advantage over traditional web hosting because they are entirely focused on helping you, the business owner, make sales. They have unlimited storage space and bandwidth, along with the ability to print out shipping labels, making fulfilling orders a snap.

In addition to all of their builtin functions, Shopify also allows you to download apps for your store. Some of the apps are free, and others cost money, but they provide all sorts of great benefits, from helping you automatically email customers after they have made a purchase to enabling customers to leave reviews on your products.

Shopify also has tools to enable you to sell your products on social media platforms, such as Facebook or Pinterest. This is great if you're wanting to integrate your social media marketing with your sales strategy.

Ultimately, Shopify is a great way to sell products online, but you need to remember it is nothing more than a sales platform. It will host all of your products just fine, and it will provide you with the tools necessary to sell, but it won't generate sales, nor will it attract people to the website just because it exists. You will need a comprehensive marketing strategy.

Dropshipping involves finding a product supplier, securing their business, and then selling their product on your sales platform, such as Shopify, without ever having to maintain an actual inventory at home. Dropshipping is the perfect way to sell high quality products to a niche consumer base without spending a fortune on an inventory that may or may not be sold.

Becoming a dropshipper is markedly more involved than just setting up a website and focusing on marketing. The road is more complex. First, you must locate a supplier who would be willing to accept orders from you. To accomplish that, you'll need to understand how a product reaches a store shelf, whether digital or in real life. Products are created by manufacturing companies. These manufacturers will then sell the products for a bulk price to wholesalers. A wholesaler's job is to find retailers who are interested in selling their product and then selling through the retailer. Wholesalers generally do not sell to the public; instead, they only work with retailers who can provide them with the best business.

If you want to become a dropshipper, you're going to be the third person on the supply chain, meaning that you are a retailer. *Your* business will become the digital storefront, showing a wholesaler's products in your shop. When a person clicks the "buy" button, they send an order to you that you will then be required to send to the wholesaler, who will package and ship the product on your behalf. The customer doesn't know that you don't own the actual products, but to them it doesn't seem any different from shopping from any other online store. The back-end, however, is very different.

A dropshipper's biggest task is finding the right wholesaler with which to do business. This can be difficult, as the world of dropshipping is rife with retailers who like to pose as wholesalers. However, with some hard work and determination, it is possible for a dropshipper to be able to find a good wholesaler who is willing to do business with them.

The second biggest challenge for a dropshipper is identifying the perfect niche to sell to. Dropshipping doesn't really have the greatest of margins primarily because you are selling products made and owned by someone else, along with the fact that competition is steep. If you can find the right niche, one that isn't particularly oversaturated by the market, you could make a killing, but it takes time and a lot of research.

Dropshipping isn't the easiest type of eCommerce, but it is economical for those who have small budgets, as you don't have to invest in things like inventory. If you don't have a large budget, but you want to get involved with eCommerce, dropshipping is a good choice.

Fortunately, Shopify works great for dropshipping, as there are plenty of apps available that can streamline and even automate the dropshipping process.

Chapter 5: Setting up Your First Shopify Dropshipping Store

In this section, you will learn about all the different steps that you need to follow to create your dropshipping store on Shopify.

Name

The first step is that you must decide on a name for your Shopify dropshipping store. Here are a couple of things that you can keep in mind while selecting a name for the store. The name needs to be simple, easy to pronounce and remember, it needs to be creative and it must be unique. You can use Oberlo's Business name generator to come up with a name for your Shopify store. You will be shown a list of business names and you can select one that appeals to you. Once you come up with a store name, you need to check whether the name is available or not. A simple Google search will help you determine whether a name is available or not.

Shopify Account

It is quite easy to create an account on Shopify for your dropshipping business. You need to visit the homepage of

Shopify and you will notice an empty field towards the top of the screen and you need to enter your email address there. Once you enter your email address, it will prompt you to create a password for your account and enter the name that you have finalized for your store. Next, you will need to fill in a couple of details about any previous experience with e-commerce and a couple of other personal details. Once you fill all this in, your Shopify account is up and running. The next step is to configure the settings to successfully launch your dropshipping account

Optimize the Settings

There are a couple of different settings that you need to optimize your Shopify account. You need to go through these instructions carefully because it relates to your store policies, mode of payment, and the shipping rates.

The first thing that you need to do is add a payment option to your store. If you don't add a payment option, then you will not be able to receive payments from customers. To do this, you need to go to the Settings section and click on the Payments tab and add the payment information you want to include. One of the best modes of payment is PayPal, so please don't forget to include this option in your payment section.

Now that you are launching your dropshipping store on Shopify; you need to include necessary store policies.

Shopify has a couple of standardized policies for privacy, refunds, and other terms of service for your store. Go to the Settings menu and click on the "Checkout" option and you will find all the above-mentioned fields on the page. Once you are satisfied with the terms of service, you need to click on "Generate" to get started.

As a dropshipper, you need to have clear policies about shipping. The easiest shipping option is to offer free shipping. If you offer different shipping rates according to the regions, then it can be quite confusing for the buyer, so it is a better idea to incorporate the cost of shipping into the price of the products you offer, so if you are offering a product for $20, instead offer it for $25 and provide free shipping. The words "free shipping" can motivate the customer to make a purchase! Go to the "Shipping" tab in the Settings menu and decide your shipping policies.

Launch your Store

Once you add all the necessary information, the next step is to launch your Shopify store. To do this, you need to click on the "Sales Channels" tab in the Settings menu and opt for the "add an online store" option. Once you do this, your Shopify dropshipping store is up and running.

Design the Store

The design of your e-commerce store is as important as the façade of a brick and mortar store. The way you present your store and your brand is quite critical. The store needs to be aesthetically pleasing and must attract the viewers. When it comes to design, there are two primary things that you need to focus on and they are the theme of your store and the logo you opt for.

Shopify offers a range of built-in themes for the store. You can find free as well as paid-for themes on Shopify, so go through the different themes available and select one that best suits your needs and budget. You need a logo for your store so that the customers can identify your brand. Creating a logo might sound like a tough job, but you don't have to be a tech-wiz to get this job done. You can always hire a graphic designer to help you with it. If you don't want to do this, then you can try Oberlo's free online logo maker to create a logo for your brand. If you want to design your own logo, then you can use different software like Photoshop or Canva. You can easily hire a professional to do this work for you from different freelance websites like Upwork or Fiverr.

Use Oberlo

Once you select the designs for your Shopify store, you need to start adding different products so that you can earn some money. To add products that you want to dropship, you must install Oberlo. Oberlo is the leading application for e-commerce store owners who want to import products to their dropshipping stores on Shopify. Oberlo and Shopify offer great integration and you can import and offer high-quality products within no time to your customers.

Once you install Oberlo, you must add a new category to your Shopify store. You can name this category according to the products that you want to sell. If you plan to start an online t-shirt business, then you can name it "clothes" or "t-shirts." Now, you can use Oberlo to search for all the products that you might want to sell. You merely need to click on the import button on the products that you want to include in your product list and all these products will be directly imported to your dropshipping store on Shopify.

You might wonder why you need to use Oberlo. Using Oberlo is a good idea because it provides you access to three types of suppliers and they are the Oberlo suppliers, Oberlo Verified suppliers, and the AliExpress suppliers. If you want to find reliable suppliers easily, then you must explore this option.

Make a Sale

Now that your dropshipping store is up and running on Shopify, the only thing that's left to do is make your first sale. You need to think about generating revenue and to do this, you need to make sales. There are different marketing channels that you can use to direct traffic to your dropshipping store like Facebook ads, Google AdWords, and email marketing. You will learn more about all this in the coming sections.

Affiliate Marketing with ClickBank

So, how can you become an affiliate marketer? There are various ways in which you can generate traffic, build your website, and select products to promote, so which method must you choose? What will work and how do you get started?

Take a deep breath, because you don't have to worry about all this anymore. In this book, you will learn about all the different steps and tips that you need to follow to become a successful affiliate marketer. Affiliate marketing is quite easy, low-risk, and doesn't cost you much.

What is ClickBank? ClickBank is a marketplace for physical and digital goods. It is quite similar to Amazon and it has a great global presence, offers secure payment options, effective tracking options, and is a great platform for affiliate marketers. In this section, you will learn about using ClickBank to become an affiliate marketer.

Step One: Find Products

You need to find at least ten products that interest you and that you want to promote as an affiliate marketer. A great thing about using ClickBank for affiliate marketing is that there are tens of thousands of products to choose from. Once you create a ClickBank account, you need to go to the Marketplace and search for different products that interest you. Make a list of these products as you continue to search for different options. Ideally, save this list in the form of a text file on your laptop or computer for future use.

Step Two: Keywords

The next step is to search for different potential keywords with the help of Google's keyword resource. To do this, you must visit Google's external keyword tool. For all the products that you selected in the previous step, you need to enter the generic keyword that you think is suitable to your product. For instance, if you want to promote a product that cures tinnitus, then the keyword that you will search for is Tinnitus and click on the Get Keywords Ideas option. Go to the "Match Type" drop-down menu and select the option "Phrase Match." You can sort this list according to the global search volume. Once you do this, you must make a list of the relevant keywords that get about 10,000 to

30,000 searches per month. Repeat this process for all the products that you chose in the previous step and you must have ten different lists with you. It is likely that a couple of these lists might be empty since not every keyword will be relevant to you. You need to be patient and don't get discouraged.

Step Three: SEO

Now, you need to check if it is possible for the keywords that you opted for to improve your ranking on Google to increase traffic to your website. Open the Google search engine and type the keywords you gathered in the previous section in the search tab. For instance, if a keyword that you gathered in the previous step is "cure tinnitus" then the phrase that you will search for on Google will be "cure tinnitus." Once you do this, Google will display the search results along with the words "Results 1-10 of about xyz" on the right side. If the xyz number is less than 100,000 then you can move on to the next step. If it is less than 100,000 then you can strike this keyword off your list.

Once you do this, you need to do another Google search and you need to type "inurl:the keyword phrase." For instance, if the keyword you are searching for is cure tinnitus, then type "inurl:cure tinnitus" and look at the results you obtain. If the number is less than 1,250 for the keyword, then it is a keeper. Repeat these steps for all the keywords you gathered in the previous step.

Step Four: Select Keywords

You need to select the keyword that you want, and you need to create a blog on BlogSpot. There are two reasons why you must opt for BlogSpot: it is easy to start a blog and the visibility of these blogs in Google search engine ranking is quite good. You must opt for a keyword with the highest search volume, the least competition numbers from the previous step, and that seems like the best fit for someone who wants to buy your product. There are no right or wrong answers here and you must pick something that meets all these three criteria.

You need to create your blog on BlogSpot, sign up and start creating content for your posts. While you are setting up a blog, please make sure that the blog's title includes your chosen keyword. Add certain characters to the keyword to make sure that it is unique. This blog will help you increase the awareness about your business and increase sales. You can also add images of the product that you are promoting as an affiliate marketer to the blog. While you are creating content about the products, don't add any fictional information. Don't overexaggerate the benefits of the product and try to be as honest as possible. You need to give a truthful and realistic description of the products if you want happy and satisfied customers for your business.

Step Five: Link building

The key to SEO is by link building and it's also the best way to increase your visibility in the search engine results for the keywords that you want to use. You must work on creating at least 5 to 10 backlinks daily. The idea is quite simple; you must get a link to your website, use the keyword of your choice in the description, and then use the keyword as an "anchor text" (the clickable text that leads you to the actual site) whenever you possibly can.

Follow these simple steps to start using ClickBank to become a successful affiliate marketer.

Email Marketing

Email marketing is a brilliant technique to market your business. You can improve the rate of conversion by emailing your customers with personalized offers. The cost of email marketing is quite low when you compare it to any of the other methods of marketing. For instance, Adore Me has a brilliant strategy for their email marketing campaigns. The subject lines, the content they use along with the visuals are all carefully thought out. A couple of subject lines that they used for their email marketing campaigns include "Drop everything. Your customized picks are waiting for you" to "you are on the list." Each of their emails is carefully crafted and encourages the reader to take some favorable action. Here are a couple of tips that can help you with email marketing.

You have probably received a ton of e-commerce emails. Why did you ever open such an email? Why did you click on the links in the emails? Perhaps the subject line caught your attention, maybe you were curious about what the email was all about, or perhaps the topic discussed was quite interesting. Email marketing is all about trial and error, so it is quite likely that you will need to test a couple of different layouts until you find something that the customer will enjoy. You can send out an email with a product list, one with good content on an interesting topic related to your niche, or it can even be a strategic combination of content and product lists.

You need to be creative when you are building your email list. You can send a quiz to the readers that will provide them a personalized recommendation at the end of the quiz. You can even host a contest or a giveaway; this by itself is a great marketing tool.

You need to segment your email list so that you can send different offers according to the preferences of your audience. You must always acknowledge and reward your loyal customers. To do this you can send them certain exclusive deals or exclusive access to your products. You need to create email subject lines that will encourage the viewer to click on the email and read through it. You will learn about growing your email list and marketing products to your email list in the coming chapters.

Before you learn about all that, you must acquaint yourself with a couple of email marketing tools that will come in handy.

Soundest allows you to send up to 15,000 emails per month and up to 2000 emails per day. This is a great tool if you have a small budget or a small email list. To increase the sales of your store, you can create campaign boosters and other welcome emails that will help establish a relationship with your customers. The other email platforms that you can use include Wheelio, Privy, and Better Coupon Box. Email marketing is essential if you want to grow your dropshipping business and increase your sales.

Facebook Advertising

Why do you need another account when you might already have a Facebook account? If you have a Facebook ad account, it helps increase the precision of your advertising campaign on Facebook. If you create an ad account, it helps you set an account through the Business Manager account, so what is a Facebook ad account? It helps you manage ads on this platform and several people can manage it. How can you create this account? Follow the simple steps given in this section to create your Facebook ads account.

The first step is to log into your Facebook Business Manager account, go to the Settings and click on the Ad Account option.

Once you do this, add the account name and link it to an advertising profile. You need to select your method of payment, your time zone, and the currency.

You can add other users who can manage this account on your behalf. If you don't have any other users in your business manager account, then you can add users to your business manager account and then use them for your ad account. If you are the only one who uses the business manager account, then you can skip this step since you don't need to add anyone. If you click on the "Add a person" option, then the popup window will ask you to add the information about the other person you want to include. Include the necessary information and assign a role of analyst or administrator to that person.

You need to continue and save your changes so that you can check the various advertising features it offers. You will need to set up a method of payment after this and that's about it. You need to enter your payment details and you can get started. If you don't want to add your payment details immediately, you can always do this after. You will have access to the targeting and audience settings, but you cannot run your campaign until you fill in the payment details.

Tips for Dropshipping

Well, it's quite amazing that you want to be a dropshipper. Now that you want to be a dropshipper, there are a couple of simple tips that you must keep in mind to improve your business. In this section, you will learn about the different tips to become a successful dropshipper.

Work on Marketing

You have the option of automating different aspects of a dropshipping business these days. Whenever you automate your business, then you have the time to focus on important aspects of business such as branding and marketing. It can be quite fun to design the logo, create content, design the graphics, and such, but if you want to start making a profit, then you need to concentrate on marketing your dropshipping business. You must spend some time on learning about the way that ads work, increase the traffic to your site, and work on converting the visitors to your store into paying customers.

When it comes to increasing your web traffic, there are two strategies that work best and these are SEO and ads. You must remember that the usual rate of conversion for an e-commerce store is around 1-2%, so if you have less than 100 visitors, then you will not be able to be profitable. The higher the traffic, the higher the rate of conversion. Usually, dropshippers tend to focus only on ads. Ads are certainly helpful if you are looking to produce instant results and increase your sales immediately, but they are effective only for a while. If you want to constantly drive up your sales in the long run, then you must focus on your SEO strategies.

SEO not only improves your rankings on search engines, but it also improves your online visibility. You can make sure that your cost of acquisition stays low while you reach a greater audience with a minimal budget, if you create blog content and start to optimize your product pages.

Not just your product pages, but you must also optimize your website for conversions. If you want to compel people to make a purchase, then you need to remember that the two factors that increase the chances of a sale are scarcity and urgency. To optimize your dropshipping website, you must increase the chances of impulse buying and add some positive customer testimonials to make the website seem credible and more appealing.

Amazing Offer

You need to create a compelling offer. You must try hard to not end up like those store owners who fail to include any offers or sales on their products. At times, a visitor needs an initial push or a slight shove to make a purchase. By offering sales or bundles you offer the necessary motivation the buyer needs to make a purchase. If you manage to present a good product with a great deal, then your rate of conversion will certainly increase.

Another offer that seems to do rather well in dropshipping is a bundle deal. Whenever you decide to create a bundle deal, you must focus on selling more units of a specific product. For instance, if you want to dropship hair extensions, then a bundle will include more hair extensions than a single unit. If your audience likes this product, then they will certainly want more of it. Here comes the tricky part: you must not only encourage the visitor to purchase something, but you must try to upsell it. Well, a combo offer always seems more appealing than a single unit.

Don't Underprice

There are a couple of platforms that allow you to underprice a product. You will be able to earn a profit if the cost of the goods you procure is reasonably close to the wholesale price and you can sell your products at market value. The aim of a dropshipping business like any other business is to be profitable. If a product costs you $5, then you need to ensure that you sell it for at least more than $15 if you want to be profitable. Don't ever underprice your products. You must consider all the aspects of business like the cost of goods, marketing expenses, and any other business expenses while pricing a product.

You must not undercut your prices because other

dropshippers are doing so. You needn't worry about undercutting the prices as long as you make sure that the price you are charging is fair and well within the market value. If you want to earn a higher return on your orders, then you must strive to increase the average value of an order.

Quality Suppliers

You will need a supplier who is reliable, offers good products, is easy to work with, and is punctual with deliveries. At times, you will come across suppliers who don't offer any of these things. While selecting a supplier, you must thoroughly vet the supplier. As a dropshipper, your rate of success is directly proportional to the supplier you work with. You will learn about finding the right supplier in the coming chapters.

Automate your Business

If you use dropshipping tools like Oberlo or Shopify, then you can automate several aspects of your business. Even if you have a full-time job or want to generate passive income, then you must come up with different ways in which you can automate your business. When you automate your business, you can free up your time and concentrate on things that do matter. There are several e-commerce tools you can use to automate, grow, and even scale your business operations. For instance, you can use Buffer to automate the posts on social media and Kit helps you automate several marketing activities like retargeting, email marketing, and even advertising.

A Presentable Website

An important aspect of a dropshipping business is your business website. The website you create must be customer-friendly and must be easy to use. The website needs to appeal to customers. Your website is as important as the physical façade of a retail store. A lot of new dropshippers don't spend sufficient time designing an appealing website. Your website is an extension of your business, so you need to include important features like a well-defined product list, important images, as well as placeholder text. Before you can launch your store, you can look at the websites of your competitors or other dropshippers in your niche for inspiration. What do their websites look like and what do they include on their homepage? Are the websites easy to navigate? Do they include their logos or images on the website? What are the different pages their websites have? What are the things that are lacking and what can you do better?

After you look at a couple of other websites, you will have a general idea of all the things that are good and bad for your business. You can imitate those aspects of their business that appeal to you and change the ones that you don't like. Your dropshipping business's website is critical for your success as a dropshipper. Your website must appeal to the viewer and it must encourage them to make a purchase.

Don't Forget about Your Competition

An important thing that you must never forget about is your competition. This tip applies to all businesses including dropshipping. You must update yourself on the strategies and marketing efforts that your competitors are making and keep a track of their scalability as well. In fact, to do this, you simply need to follow them on different social media platforms. If you do this, you can not only keep track of their business but can also track and measure their progress. Also, it will give you some ideas about the things that you can include in your marketing strategies. Doing this will help you gauge the profitability of a specific product, its demand, as well as its popularity amongst the audience. If you start paying attention to these simple details, you can improve the efficiency and the effectiveness of your business. The best way to progress is to look at what others are doing and learn from their mistakes.

Trustworthy Brand

It is your responsibility to ensure that your business does well, and you are the only one that can ensure it. You represent your business, so you need to put your best foot forward. If you work on strengthening the positioning of your brand, then you can strengthen your reputation as a leader in your niche. You must look at different aspects of your business that set you apart from your competitors.

Make a list of the various aspects of the business that you can leverage to improve the identity of your business. You must concentrate on building trust for your business; you must work on building your brand's awareness and identity amongst your target audience.

Follow these simple tips and you will be able to launch a successful dropshipping business. You will learn more about all these aspects of dropshipping in the coming chapters.

Chapter 6: Finding Suppliers

Finding a supplier for your dropshipping business isn't the easiest task, but it is the most crucial part of the whole business. If you don't find the right kind of supplier, your business will suffer immensely. There are many things to consider when it comes to finding a supplier, and there are plenty of missteps that can happen, so tread carefully. We'll break down all of the things that you need to know about finding the ideal supplier in this chapter, starting with figuring out just exactly who you want to buy from.

When the task comes to finding a supplier, you are going to have to choose the right wholesaler. We would not recommend buying from a retailer, because they already have a markup in their product, and they will be passing that markup along to you in their pricing. To make matters worse, sometimes you might end up finding retailers that try to disguise themselves as wholesalers. We'll cover how to identify scams in a later chapter.

Finding a good wholesaler will take a lot of effort. You will need to use discernment, good judgement and intuition to find a wholesaler that you can trust for high quality products. Here are a few different methods for finding a wholesaler.

Method One: Contact the Manufacturer

Manufacturers sell in bulk to wholesalers, who then sell to retailers so that they are able to make a profit. By contacting a manufacturer and asking them about who their wholesalers are, you can generate leads to trustworthy distributors. This cuts down on the time you spend searching for wholesalers and also authenticates the supplier as being legitimate, and not just a retailer in disguise.

Method Two: Use a Search Engine

Searching for a wholesaler through a search engine can be a bit of a pain primarily because of the fact that there are many websites out there who will claim to be wholesalers. Most of these websites are just posing as wholesalers but, in reality, are retailers. It will take time and energy to find the right websites, but it is possible to find wholesalers online.

Method Three: Use an Aggregator

Some web services are designed to connect dropshippers to suppliers quickly and easily. These are known as aggregators or directories. There are positives and negatives to using an aggregator. The biggest positive is that a trustworthy aggregator will be able to direct you to the right wholesaler very quickly, with very little effort required on your part. You will be able to search through a directory of wholesalers and find a wide variety of products that you can dropship.

The major drawback to an aggregation service is the fact that you are required to contribute to a monthly fee, and some might even take a percentage of your earnings. Dropshipping has fairly slim margins to begin with; volume is really the key to making money, so giving a portion of your earnings to a third party will hurt.

If you're just getting started with your dropshipping company, you might want to spend some time looking for a supplier on your own, rather than using an aggregation service. This is primarily because you'll want to be sure that dropshipping is something that you will be committing to before you invest a significant portion of money into a wholesaler directory. Besides, the skills learned from finding your own supplier can be invaluable for the future.

Finding a supplier is only one half of the inventory battle. The second half is determining if this supplier is trustworthy and efficient at what they do. You really don't want to end up doing business with a supplier that sells subpar products that break within the first week of use, nor would you want to deal with one who has terrible policies that ultimately end up harming you. So, here are some of the questions you'll need to ask about your potential supplier.

Question One: What is the insurance situation?

Insurance is important if you will be shipping expensive products, such as art or furniture. The last thing you want is to lose money because a nice vase arrived in pieces at a customer's place. You'll need to find out if the supplier insures their shipments or if that is something that you'll need to take care of.

Question Two: How good is their customer service?

If anything goes wrong in the process of sending products to the people who buy from you, it is your job to get in contact with the supplier and handle the problem. Making sure that your supplier has good quality customer service is a must. You don't want to be in a situation where you are unable to get in touch with the business due to their ineptitude. Things to look for include quick response times, professional staff who are helpful and a clear ticketing system in place.

Question Three: Are the products good?

A picture of a product isn't good enough to confer its quality. Since you will be working with a supplier long term, you will need to get your hands on some samples. Placing a sample order will give you all of the important information about the type of product being sold. You'll be able to tell whether the product is cheaply made or if it lives up to your standards. This will save you a lot of headaches in the future. Nothing is more frustrating than dealing with a customer who is upset because their product was inferior and broke upon using it.

Question Four: How efficient is the company?

How long does it take for a package to reach a customer when shipped? Does the company move quickly when they get an order, making sure to send the product out as soon as possible, or do they take their time? How does their shipping center operate? You'll need to be able to answer these questions confidently before you can select them as your supplier. The more efficient they are at handling orders, the more confident that you can be in your business. Remember, when it comes to dropshipping, all of the handling is in the hands of a third party. By doing all of your homework on the speed and response time of a supplier, you'll be able to give your customers an accurate estimate of how long it will take for their orders to arrive to their place.

Question Five: Do they require bulk ordering?

If you're just getting started with dropshipping, then you'll want to avoid suppliers who will require you to order in bulk. You may not be able to fulfill a bulk order, since you may only get a few orders at a time. Some suppliers are only interested in working with retailers who are able to bring in large orders at a time, or they use minimum order requirements as a way to keep less serious people away from them. Either way, until you get to a place where you are confident you can meet minimum orders without being stuck paying for the remainder yourself, look for suppliers that have very low order requirements.

Once you've found a prospective supplier that does well with your tests and questions, it's time for you to sign them on as your dropshipper. You must be willing to make formal contact with them, as well as make sure that they are interested in working with a dropshipper, and then work out a deal with them. This will most likely require that you make contact with management over the phone. However, just because you call and say that you are interested in dropshipping, it doesn't necessarily mean they are willing to do business with you. Most wholesalers are looking to establish relationships with businesses who are serious. You have to be able to present yourself and your company with an air of legitimacy, so the wholesaler is convinced that you're earnest about working with them. If they believe you're just looking to do this as a hobby, they would be reluctant to help, as there are far more important things for a business to do than just help a hobbyist set up a website for fun. In the next chapter, we'll talk about how to legitimize yourself by establishing your own business.

Chapter 7: The Perfect Niche Research

Product research is critical to the success of your business. You must select a great product if you want to create a business that will help you earn more than 100k per month. To select the perfect product for your dropshipping business, you need to spend some time on research.

There are three important things that you need to keep in mind while selecting a product for your dropshipping business. The product that you opt for needs to be profitable, it needs to have good demand, and it must be easy to ship. If the product that you opt for meets all three requirements, then you are off to a good start. Research is a critical aspect while you are searching for the best dropshipping products for your business. You need to immerse yourself in the virtual world of online businesses, go through different marketplaces like eBay, Amazon or AliExpress. You need to understand the product trends, the sellers who are active in a given niche, the profit margins, seller fees, and the shipping costs. If you already have a list of potential products that you can use for your dropshipping business, then you can test them with the criterion that is discussed in this chapter.

Brainstorm

If you have a list of products that you think will be good for your dropshipping business, then that's great. If you don't, then you don't have to worry.

It might seem like a basic step, but it is quite important. When you are thinking about all the different products that you can dropship, you might start to wonder if a specific product might sell online. You need to make a list of all the products that you think will sell online. At times these ideas might pop into your mind when you are thinking about a product that might solve a problem you are facing in your life. You can also get product ideas when you interact with others. Before you can select a great dropshipping product, you need to take some time and think about all the different ideas for products that might be floating around in your head. Even if the idea seems ridiculous initially, please make a list of the product ideas. You must also acquaint yourself with the products that are doing well on different marketplaces.

Social Shopping Websites

There are different social shopping websites or online marketplaces that are curated by not just users but even the tastemakers. They are quite helpful since they list the products that appeal to online shoppers. It will also help you gain insight into the kind of products that are trending and are popular before they become mainstream. These websites will save you time and you don't have to go through the thousands of product lists on your supplier's websites or other platforms like eBay or Amazon. Instead they offer a curated list of items based on current trends in the market. A couple of places that you can visit to gather this information are wanelo.co/stores, fancy.com/shop, wish.com, and etsy.com.

e-Commerce Stores

When you are thinking about the different products that you can dropship, it helps to learn from those dropshippers who are doing well in the field. You can look at the different products that the successful e-commerce stores are selling. Make a note of their listings, the photography, and the sales copy they use. All this can act as inspiration and help you come up with product ideas of your own. Going through the websites of your competitors will also help you visualize how your online store will look.

Retail Price

The price at which you can sell the product for is known as retail price. Ideally, as a dropshipper, you must opt for products that can be retailed for anywhere between $15 and $200. It might sound like quite a margin between these two numbers, but it is considered something of a sweet spot if you are interested in dropshipping. There are multiple reasons why the best dropshipping products retail for this price range and they include the following:

If you are selling a product that is perceived as being affordable, then it is quite likely that you will be able to sell high volumes of such a product. If you can sell high volumes of a product, then it increases the chances of obtaining customer feedback. Customer feedback is critical when you are building your credibility as a dropshipper. If you sell the products for less than $15, then it will significantly lower your profit margins and you will need to sell a lot of stock. On the other hand, if the product retails for over $200, then it is not considered to be affordable and it can be quite difficult to sell. Also, if you sell products for more than $200, then when you need to make any refunds, it can really burn a hole in your pocket.

So, does that mean that you can never sell over $200 per product? Well, the only time you can go higher than $150 is when you are able to sell the products with a minimum advertised price or a minimum retail price (MRP). If a product has an MRP, it means that you cannot sell the product for a price that's less than the MRP set by the manufacturer. For instance, Apple has a strict MRP policy on their products and no retailer can offer a better deal on iPhones than any of its competitors in the market. Opting for MRP products is a good idea because it prevents dropshippers from competing on the price and, instead, they need to focus on the value addition and the benefits they can offer customers. If you are just getting started with dropshipping, then it is a good idea to stick to this price limit.

Recommended Margin

The product that you want to dropship needs to offer a profit margin of at least 20-40%. The profit margin of a dropshipper is usually higher since sellers have the option to markup their retail price by 100% or even more. If you are dropshipping a product that retails for $200, then you can have a profit margin of up to 30% on such a product and you will be left with a profit of about $60 per order. If you decide to sell a product that retails for $20, then you must increase your profit margin on such a product. Remember that while you are setting your margin on the product you want to dropship, there are a couple of things that you need to take into account like packaging costs, shipping charges, marketing costs, and any other expenses that you might incur while making a sale. Therefore, it is always a good idea to opt for a product that offers a high-profit margin.

Weight and Size

Ideally, the best products for dropshipping are those that can easily fit into a shoebox. Anything larger than that and it will increase your shipping costs. You need to be mindful of the weight and size of the product if you want to be a successful dropshipper. The profit margin of your product will decrease considerably if you have a very high shipping cost. Most dropshippers tend to use ePacket as their shipping partner. ePacket is a shipping service that allows the users to quickly ship products from China or Hong Kong to the United States and over 30 other countries. If you want to use a shipping service like ePacket, you must be mindful of the size and the weight of the products. ePacket has a minimum and a maximum weight requirement for the products they ship. If you want to take up dropshipping, then you must look for products that are small, weigh less, and are easy to ship.

Moving Parts

An ideal product for dropshipping is one in which little can go wrong. You must avoid products that are fragile or fiddly, since they can easily break while being shipped and it will result in a lot of negative feedback from customers. Electrical gadgets fall into this category, especially if you are working with an unfamiliar supplier. It is a good idea to stick to products that are sturdy and can sustain the international shipping process.

Potential Repeat Business

One criterion that a lot of new dropshippers forget is that a great product means repeat business. It means that if the product is something that the customer likes, then it is quite likely that such a customer will be potentially a repeat buyer. A new concept that has become quite popular these days is the idea of subscription services. There are businesses that offer everything from luxury chocolates to feminine hygiene products that are delivered monthly to subscribers. This gives the seller a predictable monthly business. The ideal categories for this sort of business model are the products that fall into the category of health and beauty products that a person needs to purchase every time they run out. If you can successfully convert a customer, then the chances of repeat business increase, so try to check for products that you can use for a subscription service.

Supplier

Selecting the product is as important as selecting the right supplier for your dropshipping business. Without a good supplier, you cannot fulfill your orders on time and it will not help you with your business. As a dropshipper, you will potentially rely on the supplier to manufacture the product, maintain sufficient inventory, and ship it to the customer in a timely fashion. You will learn more about selecting a supplier in the coming chapters.

Low Turnover

The product that you want to dropship must be something

that will stay in production constantly. If you want to dropship a product, then you will need to invest in good quality photographs and sales copy for the product listings. If you opt for a product that will stay in production at any given time, then you can make your investment in photography and the likes last you longer. Products with a high turnover (the products that get discontinued quickly or change every couple of months) are not a good option since you will need to constantly spend money to upgrade and revamp the website and your product list.

Trials

This is an exciting step while selecting a product. If you have a dropshipping idea that made it through the previous steps and it seems like a good idea, then you need to think about whether the product will work or not. A product might look great on paper, but it needs to do well in real life as well, so the best way to test a product is to order it for a trial. It helps to test the quality of the product and the efficiency of the supplier as well.

Mistakes to Avoid

Mistakes are inevitable, and they are a part of the learning process. It is okay to make mistakes, but it will be wonderful if you can learn from the mistakes of others. In this section you will learn about the common mistakes that dropshippers make while choosing products. If you can avoid these mistakes, you will increase the profitability of your business.

You must never opt for a branded or designer product. A lot of people get tempted by big brand and designer products and they think that they can earn a lot of money by dropshipping such products. Big brands are always well known and are quite expensive and always in demand. The profit margins on such products are quite low and this makes it a very bad option for dropshippers. Unless you think you have the buying power of a huge retail store, then you must stay away from big brand products. The best products for dropshippers are generic products or private label products.

It might seem tempting to sell imitation or knockoff products since they are also always in demand, but it is a bad idea to do this. You must steer clear of all counterfeit products if you want to avoid any legal troubles and don't want to jeopardize your dropshipping business. Stay away from suppliers of those branded goods who are selling at prices that sound too good to be true.

Another common mistake that a lot of newbie dropshippers make is that they opt for highly competitive products. You might think that you have found a great product for your business since it is in demand. You must remember that others might have also thought the same and must be selling the same product. Lots of other dropshippers might be selling such products on other websites. If it is a hot product, then it must also be all over social media and you might think of it as a winning strategy. It is a bad idea to sell those products that are highly competitive. A good amount of competition in the niche you select does show that the product you opted for is successful, but it also means that you will need to compete with all those sellers who are selling the same product.

Chapter 8: Pricing Strategy

Your first big task once you are ready to launch your website is to figure out a good pricing strategy for your products. This can be a very daunting task, as you might not know exactly what price point your customers are willing to pay. Fortunately, it's very easy to adjust prices, and you can do so anytime. This gives you room for experimentation. But if you want to start out the right way, then this chapter will be useful to help you understand what is necessary to set the right prices for your products.

The first thing to keep in mind when it comes to setting prices is that your margins are going to be based on the value of the item you are selling. If you are selling high quality, expensive items, your margin will be great if you had a 15% markup. However, if you are selling inexpensive items and focusing on volume, your margins will be fairly slim. This is neither good nor bad, but it is something to consider when figuring out what your pricing strategy is going to be.

You aren't always in full control of your pricing, either. Basic economics dictates that the value of any good is worth the lowest price that it is sold for. So, if you are selling widgets for $10, and your competition is selling the identical widget for $5, your competitor is the one setting your price. Now, you can work from that range, maybe increase it to $5.50, but if you go too far from your competitor's price point, you will be left behind. No amount of company loyalty will convince a consumer to pay double for the exact same product. While this is a harsh truth, we must face it head-on. The online economy is the great equalizer. Someone can type in your product's name on Google and find the cheapest one in seconds. This means that you are always at the mercy of what the market's price point is. This is another reason why finding a niche that has a low amount of competition is valuable.

A great way to figure out what price point to settle on for a product is to go with what your supplier would recommend. They generally have a great pulse on the value of their product, and since they work with other distributors, they usually have what's known as an MSRP, or manufacturer suggested retail price. Working from that number, you can tweak it either higher or lower. Just make sure that you aren't selling below the cost of acquisition for yourself.

Negotiating to lower your purchase price from a supplier will help you get the advantage over the competition. If you can get them to drop a purchase order cost by 10%, you are then essentially making 10% more from each sale, even though the price of your product doesn't change. This, of course, requires the willingness to open a dialogue with your supplier, and they will need to trust that you are able to bring in good business for them. The better the relationship with your supplier, the better your chances of lowering your bottom line.

Another factor to consider in your pricing strategy is the season and market trends. For example, when fidget spinners briefly became popular in 2017, they were flying off the shelves. This kind of trend would signal to any savvy businessperson that it would be a good idea to increase the price, as demand was rapidly increasing. However, once the trend died out, the price should then be reduced in order to facilitate more sales. Pricing is a very active thing, and it is something that you'll need to be constantly monitoring. Don't forget that your supplier might end up changing their price structure for specific products over the years, due to a number of different factors, such as inflation, holidays and cost of raw material going up or down.

Don't stress too much about your price point, because price isn't the only reason that a customer purchases an item. While a high price can be prohibitive, and the appearance of receiving a bargain can be encouraging, customers make purchasing decisions only when they are absolutely convinced that the product would be valuable to them. If you want to be able to convince them to purchase your product, you're going to need more than just a good price. Remember, the margins are very slim in the world of dropshipping, because there are plenty of people out there peddling the same wares as you. You're going to need to utilize marketing and branding techniques in order to help a person become convinced that your items are the best bet for them. Head over to the next chapter, where we will focus on developing marketing techniques that will move your product off of your virtual shelves.

Chapter 9: Legitimize your Business

Anyone can say they are running a business, thanks to the existence of sole proprietorships. When you start doing business, you are automatically considered to be the sole proprietor of your company. This means that legally, you are responsible for everything that your company does. So, if a customer is unhappy with you and they want to bring legal issues against you, your personal life is at stake. In addition to that, wholesalers aren't particularly impressed when they see a sole proprietor, because there is no work required to get to that position.

You can avert legal problems for your personal life and legitimize your business by incorporating your company. This will protect your personal assets should you end up being sued, and it will also display to potential wholesalers that you are a legitimate business. Incorporation isn't terribly difficult, but there are different requirements depending on your state. There are some legal fees to pay, but it is a small price to pay in order to become a business owner. Not only that, but when you incorporate, you usually can find tax structures that will assist your small business when it comes to paying taxes.

You have two major options when it comes to incorporating; you can either become an LLC or form yourself as a corporation.

LLC:

An LLC stands for Limited Liability Corporation. LLCs are smaller and easier to manage than a Corporation. LLCs don't have any regulations on how management operates, nor does it have strict guidelines. You are considered to be a corporation for all intents and purposes, and you have legal insulation from personal lawsuits when it comes to company liability. As long as you maintain a strict differentiation between business spending and personal spending, legal action will most likely be against your company and not you.

Another benefit to an LLC is that you can set yourself up as a single-member, or you can have multiple members, all who have the ability to help operate the business. Most dropshippers tend to be single-member LLCs.

On top of the legal protections, LLCs experience what is known as pass-through taxation. This means that any profit or loss that you make will be claimed on your personal taxes. So, if your business reported a $10,000 loss, that would be applied to your own taxes. This can be advantageous in the beginning, since most small businesses tend to take more losses at the start.

Corporation:

A standard corporation is far more strict and inflexible than an LLC. Corporations have requirements for board members, rules for company structure and states often mandate that corporations have a certain number of meetings per year. Shares can be issues internally through a corporation, and their taxation is not pass-through. If you're looking to have a staff that will hold shares in your company, a corporation would be the ideal pick, but otherwise, stick with an LLC. They are far less complicated, and there's not much benefit to being a single person corporation.

Once you've decided how you want to incorporate, you'll need to file the paperwork to get your company recognized as its own legal entity. You have three options when it comes to incorporation:

Use an online service:

There are plenty of services online that will help you set up your corporate structure for a flat fee. Usually, these websites will take you through each step of the process and then submit the files on your behalf to the state. You'll still be responsible for paying your state fees, but these legal services tend to offer package deals and bonuses that you might not have known about without their assistance.

Do it yourself:

The cheapest way to incorporate is to simply find the paperwork on your state website and then file it yourself. You'd just need to print out the forms and then fill out all of the relevant information by hand. After that, you submit your application, pay the fees and then wait for approval. This saves you money but takes more time.

Hire a Lawyer or Accountant:

This is the most expensive option, and most of the time it isn't particularly necessary. If you are planning on creating just a straightforward LLC, then you will want to either use an online service or just do it yourself. If, for some reason, you want to have a more complicated type of filing, then you can always hire a lawyer to do so. Accountants can also assist with this; however, an accountant cannot legally give you any advice during the setup process. Either of these options costs significantly more than the two services above, and we would not recommend it unless you are looking for a very specific type of structuring that you cannot do alone.

Once you have your business incorporated, you should spend some time working on what your business plan is going to be. When dealing with a potential wholesaler, they will have questions about your direction, what kind of shop you want to run, who you are targeting, etc. If you aren't able to answer the questions definitively and quickly, it will show that you aren't ready to work with them yet. Come to the discussion fully prepared to show them that you are a worthy entrepreneur who has the foresight and the intelligence to think ahead. Remember, a good relationship with your wholesaler is of the utmost importance.

Once you have your business incorporated and a decent looking business plan, you don't have much else to do on the storefront side other than making your website live. However, after your website launches, the real hard work begins. You must then go about the task of marketing, because it will be necessary to drive people to your online store.

Chapter 10: Optimizing Your Dropshipping Website

The very first part involved with getting your dropshipping operation fully operational is to build a website. This website is going to be your central place of operations where you will sell all of your products. Remember, when you are dropshipping, you aren't selling any physical inventory from your own storage; you're selling it through a third party who will handle all fulfillment. This means that your major area of focus in dropshipping isn't going to be handling products, but rather the marketing of said products. The website is the most crucial part of your marketing because it is your link to your customers. This is where they will go to browse, order products and contact you with questions. Therefore, it is of the utmost priority that you put together the best possible dropshipping website.

In the next chapter, we'll talk more about what you actually want to be selling, so for right now, let's stay focused on the website itself. A website is a representation of your brand. The dropshipping world is highly competitive. Since there is very low overhead and the investment required to start is rather low, that means just about anyone can get started with dropshipping. On top of that, you will also have to compete with the corporate machines who produce and sell similar products to you. Without a proper brand, nothing will distinguish you from your competition. This is why it's important to prioritize creating a good website. The better the website, the better chance you have of someone buying from *you* instead of your competitors.

The first question to answer when it comes to the creation of your website is where you should host your site. There are plenty of options for online hosting, but we would recommend either Shopify or WordPress. There are both positives and negatives to each, so let's further examine each one.

Shopify:

Shopify is an easy and effective way to run your own store because it is purely designed for e-commerce. This means that you'll be getting a highly focused platform that is capable of doing just about anything that you need to become a financially viable and successful business. In addition to a great platform, easy to use website creation interface and good customer service, your Shopify website can be upgraded with paid-for apps. These apps can do all sorts of great functions, such as automating your orders or retaining customer emails for sending discounts in the future.

The downside to Shopify is that you have to pay a monthly fee to use it, and it is rather steep. The customization options are rather limited, and you don't have the total freedom that WordPress would allow. However, if you're looking for a sales platform that is easy to use and requires little programming or web knowledge, then you should use Shopify. It works well, and you can do a lot with what is provided.

WordPress:

WordPress is what's known as a CMS or "content management system." What this means is that their open source software allows you to create custom websites. WordPress is the pinnacle of customization, although if you want to customize, you have to be pretty familiar with how to use the program. If aren't terribly interested in learning how, you always have the option to hire someone to create your e-commerce site, but that does come with a higher price tag. The major benefit to this is that when you hire someone professionally, you will have a well-functioning website that responds quickly and looks fantastic.

WordPress really shines when it comes to customization. There are millions of plugins and add-ons that you can find to enhance your website, many of them free. While Shopify has a very limited amount of customization options, you can change your WordPress site however you like, since you are the owner and operator of it. You are not required to follow any specific rules or regulations when using WordPress, so you are free to do what you want.

The biggest drawback to using WordPress is that it requires a lot of knowledge and skill in order to be able to utilize it to the fullest extent. If you aren't interested in putting in the effort to get a WordPress site up and running, you would probably be better suited to using Shopify. However, the more skilled you become with WordPress, the more options in customization that you will have.

Once you have selected which website system you want to use, you'll need to focus on creating a good visual presentation for your customers. The better your website looks, the more a person will want to use it. Don't underestimate the value of visual appeal. Remember, when you're a dropshipper, nothing distinguishes you from your competition in terms of products. No matter what you choose to sell on your website, there is most likely going to be a bunch of other people who are selling that exact item. The only thing that will set you apart from the get-go is your visual appeal.

If you're just getting started with online commerce, perhaps a free theme would be better suited to your needs. There's no need to spend a large amount of capital on your first venture, because you're going to want to focus on learning the basics first. However, if you are comfortable with running online businesses or stores, then you might want to consider buying a premium theme or paying a graphic designer to create a killer web design for you. This is expensive but worth the investment if you are committed to staying in the dropshipping game long term.

Once your website serviced is selected and you have some ideas jotted down for the design, it's time for you to determine what your inventory is going to be. When you're ready, move over to the next chapter, where we will look into inventory creation and what it involves.

Understanding your Inventory

When it comes to dropshipping, inventory is handled in a very different manner. A traditional online store will have a specific inventory on hand. They will either produce or purchase items which they will then resell online. Dropshippers do things differently. They do not produce, nor do they store products; that process is handled entirely by a manufacturer, wholesaler or a retailer. Instead, the dropshipper creates a relationship with another company which produces or sells products. The dropshipper then sells those products on the third-party's behalf and pockets the profit. This means that dropshipping is a service, not a product-oriented company.

Here's a simplified example of how dropshipping inventory works. A dropshipper calls a manufacturer and negotiates a deal with which they can buy widgets for $1.00 a piece. The dropshipper then sells widgets online for $1.15 a piece. Whenever a customer orders a widget for $1.15, the dropshipper places an order with the manufacturer, paying only $1.00 and pocketing the 15 cents as profit. The manufacturer then fulfills the order and ships it to the customer.

This is the quintessential way that dropshipping works. You are a middleman, working to connect customers to your products. However, the customer does not know this about you. From their end, all they see is a website selling products. As far as they are concerned, they are buying from you and your company directly. They might not realize that you don't have warehouses full of products, and they most likely don't care about that either. All they are interested in is purchasing products.Therefore, if you want to be successful as a dropshipper, you will need to put together a strategy to establish a good, solid inventory. This is where most of the footwork for dropshipping is required. You are going to need to find the right suppliers so that you can find the highest quality products. Fortunately, there are a wide variety of suppliers that you will be able to find online, and there are even services that can help connect you with suppliers.

So, to recap what we've learned so far, a dropshipper isn't responsible for the manufacturing or storage of a product. The wholesaler or manufacturer is the one in charge of owning the actual product. Your job is to focus on finding the right fulfillment center to sell your products. There are two things to consider when it comes to inventory.

1. The Inventory Itself

You don't want to sell random, low-quality garbage that will agitate your customers. Your inventory needs to be highly focused on a niche that would attract multiple purchases from a single buyer. That means the products need to be related somehow. Your first consideration should be: what kind of products do I want to be selling? There are plenty of manufacturers and wholesalers out there, and your options are fairly unlimited. By picking one niche to focus on, you can then find the right manufacturers to assist you in fulfilling orders for that niche. For example, if you decide that you want to dropship hair products, that should be your primary focus. Don't try to sell hair products and sports accessories.

The more you focus on a single niche, the more targeted your marketing can be later on.

2. The Wholesaler

The wholesaler is the second thing to consider when it comes to creating your online inventory. A wholesaler's job is going to be to actually send the product to the customer; this means that they must have a good reputation when it comes to customer service. You wouldn't want to be involved with a manufacturer or a wholesaler who is careless with their shipping process, because you will be on the hook for their performance. Damaged products, delayed shipping and other accidents can be costly to your reputation, so make sure that you are finding the right wholesaler for the job.

Now that we have an understanding of how inventory works, we must turn our attention to deciding which products are going to be sold in your store. In other words, you are going to need to find the right niche.

Chapter 11: How to Develop Your Brand in 2019

In the world of online commerce, you are competing with millions of people for attention and sales. Both of these things are important in the online world. Without attention, you're not going to be able to gain awareness of all of your products, and without sales, your business will end up in the red. So, what makes your product any better than a competitor's? In a sea of people vying for a customer's dollar, the only thing that truly sets people apart is their brand.

A brand is a kind of identification that tells other people what your product is about. Brands are visual, conceptual and emotional in nature. They are designed to help people quickly understand what the product represents. Don't get confused here; branding isn't about what a product *does* but rather about what a product *is*.

Think about one of the most successful brands in America, or probably even the world, Coca-Cola. Coca-Cola sells a soft drink, but when they market Coke, they focus on things like togetherness, family, fun times and friendship. The beverage might be a soda, but the brand represents good times. And the world responded to that branding very positively.

Your goal should be to develop a good brand for your online store and product, so that people are able to associate your product with good values that are attractive to them. While it might seem like talking about the virtue of your product is important, that's really just advertising. Branding is about far more than just talking about your products. Rather, branding talks about what your *company* is about. People love to buy products, but if you can get them interested in your brand, then you will have a customer for life.

So, how can you get a customer interested in your brand? Well, it starts with knowing the attributes of a good brand. Let's take a look at each component of a brand, so you can learn how to appeal to customers.

Mission:

The first thing to remember about your brand is that it represents the whole picture of what your company is about. People need to have a perfect understanding of what your mission is before they are willing to get behind it. Of course, you're probably in business in order to make money; that's a given. But no one is going to support you if you say your mission is to get as rich as possible.

A mission is something that speaks to people's hearts and minds. It captures the imagination and excites them. A mission isn't about you, but it is about how your company is going to have an effect on the world at large. Don't underestimate how powerful a message can be to consumers. In the noisy world of advertisements, your mission can help set you apart.

Think about Warby Parker. They sell designer glasses online, and they are one of the more popular eyeglass companies. Yet, their mission is "Warby Parker was founded with a rebellious spirit and a lofty objective: to offer designer eyewear at a revolutionary price, while leading the way for socially conscious businesses."

Do you see how that is something you can nod your head to? Their mission has nothing to do with Warby Parker and everything to do with the world around them. They talk about a good price, a rebelliousness against the system and a desire to lead businesses in being more socially conscious. This mission is big, and when a customer learns about this desire, the company is immediately set apart from the rest of the pack. There are many places to get eyeglasses online, but there is only one Warby Parker.

Visual Identity:

Your brand needs to have some kind of visual identity attached to it. This identity includes colors, shapes or a logo. Most companies stick with one or two primary colors to put on all of their products, allowing people to readily recognize that a product is associated with a specific company. In addition to specific colors, you will also need a logo. You should probably hire a graphic designer or a freelancer to design a nice logo for your company if you don't already have one.

Uniqueness:

You also need to focus on highlighting what makes your product and your company different from all of the other products that are out there on the market. Remember, there is a vast ocean of products in the world, and they are all vying for your customer's attention. So, in order to brand yourself effectively, you need to create a strong image of being unique. Even if you are selling something that everyone else is selling, try to highlight what makes it unique to you.

Uniqueness isn't necessarily about quality, but it's about how you present your product to others. Think about medicine, for example. Most medications use the same ingredients, but they use branding to create a picture of uniqueness. They target a specific type of pain, or they have great customer service. These things are meant to help customers distinguish pain medication to be separate from the generic stuff sold in stores.

Presentation, quality and experience are the three major areas where you can work to create a great brand. You can focus on either or all of these areas, showing potential customers what makes you unique. Remember, you must always be able to answer the question: "Why should I buy from you specifically?" Work on your brand until you can come up with a sufficient answer that will motivate people to click the buy button.

Geting the right apps

As you're building up your website, you're going to need the right apps to assist you on your journey to eCommerce glory. These apps can either be free or paid, and are provided through Shopify themselves, so you don't have to worry about downloading some nasty program that can cause you problems in the future. These apps are for use with the Shopify custom store.

Boost Sales:

Boost Sales allows for you to implement upsells during a customer's checkout phase. In addition to this, there are a variety of options that you can implement that will allow you to entice and excite your customers to purchase products from you. With things like smart recommendations, a sales motivating system and crossselling products as bundles, this is a great add-on if you're looking to sell a lot in a short amount of time.

Audience Push:

This great app allows you to add people who buy from your store to your Facebook Advertising account's custom audience list. We'll be covering Facebook advertising in the next chapter, but just know that Audience Push will allow you to retarget customers who have purchased from you later on, boosting the chances of getting repeat business.

Receiptful:

Receiptful allows you to customize the receipts that you send out after someone has purchased your product. This customization allows you to maintain your brand identity and also to even put in custom codes for discounts later on, increasing the chance of repeat business.

Persistent Cart:

Persistent Cart is fairly simple; if a customer leaves your website with products in their cart, when they return, the products will still be there. This allows for customers to quickly be reminded of what they were wanting to buy, and it reduces the chances of them forgetting what they had wanted to get.

Tidio Live Chat:

Sometimes, a customer might have a question, but sending an email isn't particularly satisfying because it will require some time before a reply arrives. However, with live chat, a customer can quickly have their questions answered and receive the satisfaction of a good customer service experience. Tidio allows customers to quickly type a question into a chat bar, and you'll receive the question immediately. Then, you can reply without delay, increasing your customer's overall satisfaction and hopefully locking down a sale right there.

Chapter 12: Email Marketing Strategies

Now that you have an email list in place, you need to concentrate on email marketing, so what is the most successful email marketing strategy that you can use? Did you know that over 200 billion emails are sent out every day? Well, that's a whole lot of competition that you need to worry about. Also, keep in mind that those email numbers keep increasing every day. Therefore, it is quintessential that you know how to go about email marketing to reach your target audience and retain their attention.

Establish your Goals

You cannot create a marketing campaign without setting certain goals and the same applies to an email marketing campaign as well. If you want to run a successful email marketing campaign, then you need to think about the goals that you want to achieve. Your goal can be to welcome new subscribers, nurture the relationship with existing customers, increase the rate of engagement, re-engage with subscribers, or even segment your subscribers. According to your goals you will be able to design the campaign. Not just that, your goals will also dictate the kind of content you can include in emails.

Types of Emails

You need to understand that there are different types of emails you can send. Usually, they are grouped into three categories and they are promotional emails, relational emails, and transactional emails. Promotional emails are the ones that you will send when you want to inform readers about different promotional offers you are running. The relational emails allow you to give subscribers their weekly updates or any other relevant information that helps maintain good customer relationship. Transactional emails are the ones that you will send if you have to confirm a subscription, confirm an order, or anything related to any transaction related to your business. Transactional emails are the response to any action that the subscriber takes on your website.

Your Audience

If you have been into email marketing for a while, then you will know your audience. If you are just getting started with email marketing, then you will need to take some time to get a general understanding of your audience. You need to understand your audience since this is the primary criterion that describes the kind of content you can use. It is quite easy to gather all the necessary information that you need about your audience. You can use the metrics from social media profiles and Google Analytics to get a general understanding of your audience. These tools will provide you with data about different metrics like the demographics of your audience, their interests, location, and such. Gather all this information and analyze it. When you do this, you will have a rough idea of the kind of content you can create for your emails.

Use Technology

There are different email marketing tools that you can use to create a successful email marketing campaign. When you are selecting a tool to work with, look for something that offers automation, provides templates, and helps with campaign creation. The service you opt for must seamlessly integrate with any other software that you use like WordPress; it must help you segment your audience and must provide you with a good analysis of your campaigns.

Opt-ins

You need to have an email list if you want to run a great campaign, so to attract more people to join your email list, you need to have a bunch of great opt-ins. You need to have an attractive sign-up form that encourages readers to sign up for your email group or subscribe to your emails.

Emails and Follow-ups

Once you are aware of your goals, the type of emails and the audience you need to work with, you need to plan your email marketing campaign. You need to plan the kind of emails you want to send. The content that you will include in your emails is quite important, so don't just send the readers a random template with a generic mail. Instead, you need to spend some time creating an attractive email that makes users stick around and not click on the unsubscribe button. You must not only plan for the emails you want to send, but also think about the follow-up emails to send.

Subject Line

The subject line that you use for your emails is quite important. The subject line is the first thing that the viewer will see, so you need to make sure that it is something that will encourage the reader to open the mail and go through it.

Copy

The next thing that you need to focus on is the email marketing copy you want to use. You need to create a copy that will motivate the reader to read on. It is a good idea to keep the copy short, crisp, and avoid any sales pitches. You need to make the person comfortable before you get down to pitching. It is always a good idea to make the email personalized and the best way to do this is by addressing the subscriber by their name. Also, don't forget to include a call to action in your emails. What is the action that you want the reader to perform after reading the email? The call to action needs to be easy and simple to understand.

Email Marketing Design

If you want to run a successful campaign, then you need to concentrate on the email design. If the email looks terrible, then it will reflect rather badly on your business and it might make the reader stop reading. A lot of people tend to check their emails on their mobile devices, so you need to make sure that your email template is responsive to the device it is being viewed on and can optimize itself immediately.

While writing the copy for your email, make sure that you don't include too many pictures. Usually, most email users tend to disable the images option, and when they do this, the reader cannot view the images you use in your email, so it is a good idea to stick to text.

Test

Sending out your first email is the first step to running a successful email marketing campaign. To optimize the results you receive from this campaign and to improve your future campaigns, you need to collect data. You need to test everything that's a part of your email marketing campaign. It means that you need to test everything from the design of the email, the template you use, the copy you write, subject lines, and the call to actions you use. You must also experiment with different timings and segments of your audience. Gather all the data that you can from all this and keep track of it. After a while, it will help you find the best practices to optimize the results of your email marketing campaign.

Get People to Read Your Emails

All the different strategies that you use for email marketing will not matter if you cannot get people to read your emails. Even if you have an extensive database of email addresses, what good do you think it will do your business if you cannot get anyone to read your emails? Well, the answer is that it does you no good, so in this section you will learn about the different ways in which you can make the reader read your emails.

Deliver value

The emails that you send need to be short and simple to understand. If the emails are lengthy, then you will certainly lose the interest of the reader. With emails it is all about quality and not quantity. You can use the emails to extend any offers to the reader that they will not receive otherwise. A good sales pitch is like a greased slide at a playground; your reader will smoothly slide down without any resistance whatsoever. The opening sentence of the email needs to be short, crisp, and to the point. It needs to pique the reader's curiosity and must make the reader want to read through the email. You need to use your brand voice to convey the information that you want to in a clear and informative manner.

Compelling Subject Line

The subject line of your emails must be such that it compels the reader to open the emails. The subject line needs to be precise and descriptive. The subject line must not bore readers and must not be difficult to understand. When you are crafting the subject line, you can use a couple of the tips given here.

The subject line can include ambiguous statements that make the reader curious. The subject line must address a relevant concern of the subscriber. It needs to show some value or create a sense of urgency. It can perhaps trigger an emotional response with a bold and true claim.

Write the Emails Together

If the email is a part of a drip campaign, then try writing them all at once. If you do this, then you can maintain a consistent style of writing and can avoid any choppy work. You can lead the reader through different stages of a sales funnel smoothly if you write all the emails in one go.

Build a Mailing List

Once you have finished setting up your store and getting your apps in place, it's time to start focusing on how to market your website and your product. Remember this simple rule: it doesn't matter how great your product is; if you don't market it, no one will find it.

This is a very simple rule that is worth guiding your entire marketing policy. Sometimes, we can get too caught up in how interesting and well-made our products are, to the point where we erroneously come to the conclusion that all we really need is a good product. However, there are extreme limits when it comes to things like word-of-mouth marketing. You need something stronger. In the next few chapters, we'll be covering differing methods of marketing, starting with the mailing list.

The mailing list is the single most powerful marketing tool that you should have in your arsenal. If you aren't working on building a mailing list, then you are going to be losing out on the ability to send specials, offers and reminders to a potential customer base. Essentially, the mailing list comprises of a list of people who have *voluntarily* handed their email addresses over to you. You are then free to email them as often as you like.

You need an email list, because no other marketing system is as useful and direct as an email. All other forms of advertising rely on people noticing your ads and clicking on them, but an email arrives directly in their inbox and begs to be opened. There is no hoping to catch attention, because unless they delete it without looking at it, they will read it, even if it's just for a moment.

Starting an email list isn't too difficult. There are plenty of different and unique services that you can utilize when it comes to building your mailing list. The one we would recommend would be MailChimp, because it's intuitive, easy to use and free until you reach over 2,000 subscribers. MailChimp also lets you send custom campaigns and track the amount of people who have opened, read and clicked on links within your emails. This kind of data is valuable because it allows you to know just how many people are engaging with your promotions.

Setting up an email list is easy, but getting emails on that list is the hard part. There are a variety of different ways that you can generate emails, but you'll want to be careful. Focus on getting quality emails, also known as leads. A quality lead is someone who is in your target demographic and would be interested in buying your product. One quality lead is better than 10 emails because you want to find emails that have a big chance of buying products from you. This means that you should develop email list building patterns composed only of high quality leads who will actually purchase things from you. If you have 1,000 poor quality leads, you can email them until you're blue in the face, but you'll get lucky if even one person buys. However, if you had 100 high quality leads, they might purchase far more because they are part of your target demographic.

So, if you are wanting to gain emails, you're going to need what is commonly referred to as a lead generation system. This means that you have some kind of attraction program in place that will gather leads for you. People don't just give their emails away; rather, they are cautious with their information until they come across a deal that is beneficial to them. Then, they are willing to trade their email in exchange for some kind of item.

The item can be a free product, a discount code, an eBook or any other thing of value. It's got to be valuable enough to encourage a potential customer to sign up, but not too valuable that it would attract people outside of your target demographic. For example, if you sold knitting patterns, you could have a free eBook with knitting patterns, which in turn would attract people who were into knitting. But if you were to offer a free crocheted hat, many people who find the product valuable but have no interest in knitting patterns would sign up for it. This costs you a lot of your money and, worst of all, doesn't provide you with much value.

One of the most tried and true methods of lead generation is the free eBook giveaway. You simply offer the eBook on your website in exchange for an email address. This is one of the best ways to start a relationship with a potential customer, because the eBook will give them an opportunity to sample some of your work. If you aren't much of a writer, you can always hire a freelancer or a ghostwriter to make something for you. The book doesn't have to be really long; it just has to add some kind of value to your potential client's life.

Promotions, contests and giveaways are all great ways to generate leads as well, but you should always make sure that they are only appealing to your target demographic. Going outside of your demo is a costly endeavor and is ultimately a waste of time. Instead, keep your focus on finding quality leads by developing good giveaways or, as they are called, lead magnets.

You might be wondering how exactly people are going to find out about your giveaways. You can have the best lead magnet in the world, but if people aren't landing on your website, then how are they going to hear about it? And this is where we will be moving on to the next chapter, where we will take a look at one of the best marketing tools ever invented: Facebook advertising.

Chapter 13: Facebook Advertising For Products in 2019

Advertising can be a scary thing, especially if you aren't familiar with how marketing works. Oftentimes, there are a lot of assumptions that we make about marketing, like "it costs a fortune to advertise," or "I need a professional marketing team to market well." These assumptions usually come from the fact that we are still in a transitional economic stage, moving into a digital world that is very different from the old ways.

But have no fear! Facebook advertising is here to help you get your product shared with the masses at an affordable price. The Facebook advertising model is brilliant because it is extremely targeted. When a person is using Facebook, the system begins to learn information about this person. It learns their habits, their likes, interests and other relevant facts that make advertising easier. While some people might be concerned about the privacy issues behind these algorithms, it simply comes with the territory of using social media.

These habits, behaviors and interests are entered into a database. An advertiser can create an ad that targets specific types of behaviors, such as knitting, and when the ad runs, it will run in front of the people to whom it would be most relevant. This is extremely targeted advertising and allows for you to have an intense and specific focus when it comes to finding people in your target demographic. Instead of shooting an ad out in front of thousands of random people of all different interest groups, Facebook will only display your ad in front of those who are most likely to click on it.

In fact, Facebook's system is so efficient that by today's standards, it is considered to be the most powerful advertising system ever made. And it is with Facebook advertising that you are going to have the opportunity to put your lead magnet in front of people. You can also advertise specifically for your product as well with this system. But you should prioritize your lead magnet because over the long run, it will make advertising costs cheaper.

Look at it this way. If you spent $1 to obtain 1 email address through Facebook, you can market to that person as many times as you'd like directly through email for a cheap or nonexistent cost. This works better than just focusing on marketing products through Facebook. If you have a big enough budget, you should be doing both, but if you want to know which one to prioritize, we would suggest the email list builder because it will create a stronger network for you down the road.

So, how do you get set up with Facebook ads? It's simple enough; all you need to do is set up an advertising account on Facebook, putting in the relevant details as necessary. From there, you can start creating an ad. Let's look at each basic step needed to create a Facebook ad.

Step One: Have a graphic

Ads are displayed on a person's Facebook page as they are scrolling down their feed. The average person will spend about 50 minutes a day on Facebook, leaving plenty of time for them to notice an ad or two. Your ad needs to have a good graphic in order to catch people's attention. Making Facebook graphics isn't too difficult; you can use a drag and drop website like Canva to assist you with creating ads, or if you really need a good graphic, you can always hire someone to do one for you.

There are constantly changing rules to how graphics can look, so make sure you check with Facebook's rules to see what is or isn't allowed on a graphic.

Step Two: Build an Audience

This is really the most crucial part when it comes to carefully crafting a Facebook ad. Your audience is essentially the ideal person who looks at your ad. This is where Facebook will be able to determine, with algorithmic processes, where your ad will actually pop up. Chances are, it's going to take some time to figure out the best audience. You'll notice, as you select interest groups, Facebook will give you a projected number of people who it could potentially reach. The number could range anywhere from 100,000 to several million. You don't want an overly broad audience, as they might not be too interested in whatever it is that you are selling. Instead, try to put as many behaviors, interests and likes as you can to shrink the size of the audience.

Once you have a decent sized audience that isn't too big, you will be given a number of impressions that your ad will make per day. This is a projection of how many people will like or click your product page. These projections are based on how much money you are putting into the ad.

Step Three: Determine Ad Placement

Here you can determine where your ad will be seen. This is a crucial decision as well; if you don't choose the right places, the ad could be a real waste of time. You can choose whether you want the ad to be automatically placed or if you want certain restrictions, such as preventing the ad from running on Instagram. You would do this if you were advertising something that you didn't want to be on Instagram, such as PC software. There's not much of a reason to sell software to people who are browsing on Instagram, because they won't be on their computers but rather their phones.

Step Four: Determine Budget and Schedule

Facebook utilizes something known as Pay-Per-Click. This simply means that you don't pay for your ads until someone clicks on it, moving them somewhere else. This means that your budget will have a maximum and a minimum number of clicks that you can generate. You want people clicking on your ad, so it makes sense to try and go for the highest amount that your budget will allow.

A budget will run for a set number of days, based on how you schedule it. If you want to set a $50 budget to run for 7 days, you might end up with a statistic like 7-10 clicks per day. $50 will be the maximum that your budget will run for and when you hit the final day, your ad will end its run. Now, it is possible for clicks to be cheaper or more expensive, but this is based on the advertising space being utilized. We won't get into it too much, but just know that the price of ad space is based on the amount of bids being done by other companies. Fortunately, there is plenty of room for everyone in the Facebook advertising game, but if you have a very popular demographic and a popular niche, then the price of ads could be higher than anticipated.

Step Five: Review the effectiveness of the ads

Once your ad has finished its run, you should spend some time analyzing the effectiveness of the ads themselves. You'll want to examine what the conversion rate is. A conversion simply means that a person who clicked on your ad engages in the behavior that you wanted. So, if it's an eBook giveaway, a conversion would be after a customer signs up for your mailing list. If you are linking them to a product, a conversion would be a sale.

No stat is more important than conversions. These are what's known as key performance indicators, and they will tell you how well your company's advertising is doing. No number of clicks, traffic or likes can amount to a conversion. So, don't focus too much on traffic; instead, try to focus on increasing the conversion rate as much as possible.

Advertisement Sets
In this stage, you need to develop advertisements based on your audience's interest, demography, occupation, types of posts they read, pages they have commented on, their purchasing frequency, personal interest, and their life

events. You can use a tool called 'Facebook Audience Insights' to make this process easier. You need to use this tool if you want to make an advertisement that will generate revenue. For instance, if you sell sports accessories, you must develop different advertisements for your customized audience, a set for people who have purchased from your website and for the people who live close to your store.

Advertisements

This is the final stage. An advertisement is the most relevant and narrowest combination of the targeted audience and the most useful objective. This is where you will create your live advertisement. For every part of the advertisement set, you must mix and match different descriptions, images, and multiple logos. You can then use these combinations to see which one will work best. You must always remember to run the A/B tests. A simple change in image or color can boost the rates by at least 90 percent.

How to Target the Right Audience

Studies show that if you do not target the right audience, you will run your dropshipping business into the ground. If you have conducted sufficient research on the dropshipping business, you know that your audience matters.

Interest, Occupation and Demography

It is obvious that an eighty-year-old man and a high school girl will not like the same Facebook pages. You can use 'Facebook Audience Insight' to distinguish your target audience by using their occupation, age, recent life events, hobbies, purchasing frequency, and interests. Your audience's interests include the types of posts they like, the groups they belong to, and the pages they visit.

If your company sells kitchen appliances, Facebook will target the users in the same area who have recently purchased kitchen appliances. It will also give you a list of people who have some interest in kitchen appliances. You can then target the potential customers. This is what you need if you want to establish a dropshipping store.

Geography

When your circle is concentrated, you will succeed in the dropshipping business. When you advertise your products on Facebook, you must first start with the location. If you are a retailer in Asia, you cannot expect to sell products in Australia unless you start an online store. You must always target potential buyers in the areas where you know you can deliver products on time.

Custom Audiences

Apart from posting your advertisements to targeted audiences, you can also customize your viewer list. You can obtain the email addresses of your viewers from positive reviewers, previous customers, and people who have contacted you for specific products.

Budget

It is true that money matters. You do not want to waste a single penny when you are starting a dropshipping business. Experts suggest that you always go slow. Instead of investing a large sum of money in your business at a single time, you must only campaign a small amount of money. You must follow the growth and then invest accordingly. If you use the 'Facebook Advertising Tool,' you can either make a one-time investment or pay for advertisements daily. You must always test new things. You will lose some money initially, but you will make more money than you will lose. You must learn the lessons and remember that you must only focus on marketing. You do not have to worry about packaging, inventory, or shipping. You must pull your socks up and try new things. You must not worry if you lose some money. It is true that the daily budget is lower for obvious reasons, but experts recommend that you go for the 'Lifetime Budget' until you learn how to invest. When you pay daily, you will spend more when compared to the amount you spend on the 'Lifetime Budget.' It is a good idea to choose the lifetime budget if you want Facebook to spend the money you have invested only on advertisements. Facebook will spend your money in the following ways: on the basis of impressions (CPM) or clicks (CPC). With the CPC, Facebook will generate advertisements for you and target relevant users. With the CPM, Facebook will deduct money from your investment when someone clicks your advertisement at least a thousand times. The 'Facebook Advertising Tool' will allow you to include any other discount coupon if you want.

You can place your advertisement on Facebook in the following order:

Desktop News Feed

Mobile News Feed

Instagram

Audience Network

Desktop Right Column

Statistics show that the first two options always generate the maximum amount of traffic. This means that you must avoid the desktop right column.

Creating and optimizing Ads

Facebook offers multiple advertising options and you don't always have to promote a single post. You can select the type of ad based on different objectives. One of these objectives can be to boost or promote a specific post. There are different options that include promoting your Facebook page, directing others to your dropshipping website, increasing the rate of conversion and also encourage users to claim any offer that you provide. Once you select the objective of your campaign, then you can select different options regarding the targeted audience, budget, and the creatives that you want to use for your ads. If you select an objective, it will help meet your advertising goals. There are three placement options available and they are your desktop feed, the column on the right side of the screen, and the mobile newsfeed. The default option is that all these three options will be selected. If you don't want your ad to be displayed in any of these locations, then you need to click on the remove button that's present next to the location name. Usually, people tend to spend a lot of their time and money on Facebook Ads without understanding the way it works. If you want to avoid doing this, then you need to ensure that the ads perform according to the objectives that you have set for yourself.

In this section, you will learn about the various things that you can do to create and optimize the Facebook Ads you create.

Appropriate Editor

Ads Manager and the Power Editor are the two tools that Facebook offers to create ads. When you are trying to decide between these two options, you need to consider the size of your business and the number of ads you want to run at any given point of time. The Ads Manager option usually suits the needs of most businesses. If you are a large advertiser and want to have precise control over all your campaigns, then you must opt for the Power Editor tool.

Objective

The Facebook Ads Manager helps you design an advertising campaign, but you need to set some objectives for this tool to effectively fulfill this objective. There are ten pre-installed objectives that you can choose from and they include clicks to website, page likes, app installations, app engagement, website conversions, page post engagement, video views, offer claims, event responses, and local awareness. Whenever you select an objective from this section, it helps Facebook serve your needs better and improves the overall efficiency of your advertising campaign. If you want to increase the traffic to your website, then merely click on that option from the list of objectives. Once you do this, then Facebook will ask you for the URL that you want to promote. If you want to use any automated marketing software, then you need to ensure that you are using URL and UTM parameters to track the traffic as well as conversions.

Select your Audience

If you are using Facebook ads for the first time, then you will need to try a couple of different targeting options until you find one that works well for you. Facebook offers different targeting criteria that you can use. If you are not too sure about the kind of audience you must target, then take some time to think about your objectives. If you want to increase traffic to your website, then you must focus on all those who will be interested in what you are offering. If you want to build awareness of your business, then it makes sense to create an ad that will appeal to the general audience. The different factors that you must consider while creating an ad are the location, gender, age, interest, language, finances, life events, behaviors, connections, and work of the audience.

You also have the option to select a custom audience. If you opt for a custom audience, then it gives you the option to target all those present on your business's contact list like the people who visit your website or app users. Once you find a group that you think will react favorably to your ads, then the next step is to save that selected audience.

Budget

There are two types of budget that Facebook offers for its ads and they are the daily and lifetime budgets. If you want to run an ad continuously throughout the day, then you must opt for the daily budget option. By using this option, Facebook will pace your daily budget according to the number of times you want the ad to be displayed. The minimum budget that you can set is $1 per day. If you want to create an ad that will run for a specific period of time, then you must opt for the lifetime budget option. Facebook will pace the entire budget of the ad according to the lifecycle of the ad. You must decide the schedule for the ad. For instance, do you want the ad to run immediately or do you want it to run during a specific period? You have the option to customize the ad so that it runs only during a specific hour in any day.

You must select if you want to bid for your objective, clicks, and impressions or not. The way the ad will be displayed is based on this decision. When you do this, you will only pay for a specific ad that will be shown to your target audience. Facebook tends to control your maximum bid when you are using Facebook ads, or it does so usually. If you don't want this, then you must opt or manual bidding. This option gives you free rein over the amount that you want to spend per action that is complete. You must also select the delivery option. There are two delivery options available and they are standard and accelerated delivery. If you want your ad to be shown throughout the day, then opt for standard delivery. If you want your ad to reach your target audience quickly, especially if the content of the ad is time-sensitive, then opt for the accelerated delivery option.

Nathan Michaud
Make Your Own Marketing Strategy

Now that you have a clear picture of how Facebook advertising really works and you know what's needed to set up an email list, you should be ready to create your first marketing strategy. Now, marketing is a massive undertaking, and you will not do it right the first time. But that is perfectly okay, because marketing is all about learning what works and what doesn't. In the world of online marketing, failure is perfectly fine, because learning what doesn't work is just as valuable as learning what does work. Nothing is a true failure if you learn from it.

With that in mind, you're going to need to take some time to sit down and write up a comprehensive approach to marketing your product. If you wing it or just haphazardly plan for the future, you will be in for a sore disappointment. Marketing shouldn't be random or based on how you feel, but it should be based on a plan.

Now, you might be a smaller organization, and you may not have a crazy big budget. But that's okay. As long as you have $5 bucks, you can market. The return won't be wild, of course, but even slow gains are better than no gains. Let's break down the marketing plan into a series of steps. Follow each step and write down your approach, creating one seamless marketing strategy to follow.

Step One: Develop a lead magnet

As talked about before, you're going to need a good lead magnet. Ask yourself this: "what would get my customer excited to receive in exchange for their email?" Would it be a guide? A physical product? If you aren't sure what to do, that's fine; take a look at our list of potential lead magnets

- Checklist
- Video course
- How-To eBook
- Coupon
- Free trial
- Contest entry
- Product giveaway
- Webinar
- Recipe
- Exclusive Blog Post

Step Two: Determine monthly advertising budget

If you want exposure, then you'll need to shell money out on ads. This is just how the world works. Yes, there are plenty of different organic methods that exist that can assist you in your quest to reach as many people as you need, but organic isn't nearly as targeted. Organic marketing's inefficiency means that you will need to set up a monthly advertising budget. Allot whatever you feel comfortable with to a monthly budget, even if it's only for the current month you are in. If your budget is in constant flux, then it's fine to go month to month and adjust your budget on what you can afford, but it's never a good thing to *not* have a budget.

Step Three: Create Ads and allocate budget

Your ads should have multiple goals based on what you are trying to achieve. You will also need to allocate money based on each ad. If you're short on cash, prioritizing ads that will have the maximum short term return isn't a bad idea, so you would put more of a budget into product advertisements. If you have enough cash but are low on leads and traffic, then maybe put more money into awareness campaigns.

When you create an ad, you should always have a goal for that ad. The goal could be simple, such as getting a conversion, generating a lead, or just building awareness for your product. But you should never just release an ad without having some kind of purpose behind it. Even test ads should be released with an extreme purpose.

Step Four: Create newsletters

You should sit down and create a stack of newsletters, promotional emails, etc. for your email campaigns. Make enough to last you a few months of advertising. They should be functional, interesting and well-made. If you aren't sure how to design a newsletter or promotional email, you can either hire someone to make them for you or work on learning it yourself.

Step Five: Plan an email schedule

Once you have leads, you should sit down and come up with a series of campaigns and an email schedule. You can set up emails so that they send in the future, so you won't have to remember to send out promotionals month to month. When it comes to sending emails, there is no exact science to how many you should be sending out, so rather than give you a hard number, we will give you a principle: **every email that you send should add value to the customer.**

Adding value is something as simple as telling them about a new product and how great it is for them, or something nice, like sending coupons or discounts. If you are sending emails that provide nothing to the consumer, they will be very quick to unsubscribe, which could have been avoided. Put together a schedule, and be sure to figure out things, like product announcements or sales, ahead of time.

Step Six: Analyze the numbers

Once you have run your lead generation system, your Facebook ads and your email campaigns, spend a few hours poring over the numbers to determine how effectively things are going. Chances are, you might end up seeing numbers that aren't incredible. This is okay, because you're learning what doesn't work. Throw out poor performing ads or emails and start fresh. You can start over as many times as you need. You just need to get it right once or twice, and then you can build up from there.

Step Seven: Maintain a schedule

If you run your business, marketing is always going to be a part of your life. Unless you are willing to spend the money on hiring a marketer, which isn't always an option for the smaller businesses, you will have to maintain a marketing schedule. This means that you must have it marked on your calendar to put at least a few hours a week into marketing. If you don't, you will end up in serious trouble over the long run. Remember, a business doesn't succeed because it sells the best product, but because it markets properly. The best product in the world isn't going to catch fire unless people know about it first. Your job is to help as many people know about it as possible. Then and only then will you find true marketing success.

Chapter 14: Getting Started With FBA

So, you've done the research on the numbers, you've seen the potential for making money, now what? Well, we need to get you set up and ready to go with using Fulfillment By Amazon. The setup process isn't particularly hard, so let's walk you through each step so that you can start selling.

Step 1: Get a seller's account

Chances are, you probably have an Amazon account of some type already. If that's the case, then you're going to need to set up a seller's account. Searching for Fulfillment by Amazon will take you to the official FBA page. This will be the portal that will take you to the registration page where you can get started. You'll need to have a seller's account first, and after you register that account, you will be able to set up your FBA account as well.

Step 2: Input Relevant Details

Once you have gotten your seller's account set up, you must then enable FBA. Fortunately, this is an easy enough process to do. Just follow the instructions provided by Amazon and in a matter of minutes, you should have the capacity to be working with FBA. It's important to note that all of the details that you input must be relevant and true. Amazon will be keeping track of your information for tax-related purposes, so don't make the mistake of inputting false or inaccurate information. Come tax time, you're going to need all of your ducks to be in a row.

Step 3: Get ready to use FBA.

Once FBA is all set up, all you have left to do is start shipping your inventory to them. But what exactly do you have to ship to them and what are they looking for? Well, that is one of the most important parts of FBA. So, let's move on to the next chapter, where we will discuss what you will be selling.

Product Acquisition

Okay, so you've been figuring out what kind of product you want to be selling online; now, you've got to start working on acquiring that product. Fortunately, there are a lot of different strategies that you can utilize to assist you in making the most amount of profit off of these products.

Remember, the name of the game here is profit. No matter how much you sell an item for, you have to make more money than you originally spent on the product and the shipping costs. You must keep this in mind when you start to figure out how you are going to approach gaining product. How can you get the highest quality products for the lowest price?

In this chapter, we'll look at a few different ways that you can acquire product for cheap. Some of these strategies rely on a bit of luck and good fortune, while others are more stable. Ultimately, it is up to you how you want to approach the market.

Product Acquisition Strategy 1: Take Advantage of Clearance

The clearance section of any store can be your best friend. A lot of times you will find perfectly good products on sale in any retail store because the product simply wasn't moving off of the shelves. The products can vary, but if you are looking for items to snag for upwards of 75% off, this is a great strategy. By regularly hitting clearance racks at your preferred big box stores, you can load up a product that you could easily turn around and sell for regular retail prices, reaping a hefty profit. The best part of this strategy is the fact that you are also saving a lot of money on inventory costs, since you are purchasing them at a discounted rate.

The downside is that you won't be able to stockpile a lot of similar products unless a specific product is heavily being eliminated by retailers, and then you might need to make sure that there is nothing wrong with the product. If you're working to sell OTC drugs, you'll also have to check to make sure there hasn't been a recall on the drugs or if they expire soon. You never want to send out a subpar product through FBA to make a quick buck; that will cost you a lot in the long run.

Product Acquisition Strategy 2: Coupon Your Way to Victory

Coupons and special discounts can be an excellent source of finding top quality products at a discounted rate. Many stores and retailers send out a lot of coupons each month as a way to drum up sales and business, so by taking advantage of a 30% off coupon on an expensive item, you can flip it and make yourself a nice 30% profit when you sell it for full price on Amazon. Now, the gains here aren't amazing, but if you steadily develop a strategy of couponing to get products that are more in demand, you will also experience a faster turnaround. A product sold quickly for a 15% profit is better than a product that just sits on the shelf and does nothing.

Of course, you must make sure that you are able to acquire products that you know will move off the shelf. Over time, you will start to get an understanding of what products sell quickly and which ones stay in one place for too long. Make sure that whatever you are buying, you know that someone would happily pay to purchase it. This means when it comes to tech, resist buying products that are older or obsolete. There might be a place for selling old tech to a niche market, but a lot of the time, people aren't interested in buying old technology.

Product Acquisition Strategy 3: Find Surplus Stores

A surplus store is somewhere that holds an excess amount of product that other retailers ended up having on their hands. This could be caused by all sorts of different scenarios: the company might have overbought a specific product and now just wants to recoup some of its losses, or most likely, the surplus store purchased the items at a serious discount and now is flipping them for half the regular retail price.

Chances are there are quite a few surplus stores in your city. They could deal with all sorts of different products, so you could make a habit out of regularly hitting them for extremely cheap products and then flipping them online for a great profit. Anytime that you can find a name brand product, chances are it will sell for higher online. Always be sure to check the prices and see how Amazon prices compare to the current prices that you are looking at on the shelf, and then account for how much time will go by before you can reasonably get the product shipped out.

Product Acquisition Strategy 4: Online Sales

You don't always have to leave the comfort of your own home if you want to get product for selling through FBA. In fact, thanks to the prevalence of online retail, you can find a great amount of cheap product without ever having to put your shoes on. All you have to do is sign up for a bunch of different online newsletters for various retail companies and let the discounts come right to you. Then, you order online, and once it arrives, take the brand new package and wrap it right back up, sending it straight to a fulfillment center.

The benefit here is that you can quickly access a lot of information with minimal effort. Just find the websites that you like, look for their daily deals sections and make sure that it is the type of product that you are looking to sell; then, you're good to go. No hassle, no muss, no fuss. You could even make a daily habit of checking prices online each day to see if there's anything that is on a special sale.

Product Acquisition Strategy 5: Garage Sales/Antiquing

This method isn't the best strategy when it comes to making bulk sales online, but if you are inclined, you could spend your Saturday mornings looking for garage sales in the hopes of finding a valuable product for cheap. One of the best benefits behind these kinds of sales is the fact that you can haggle with the owner. Most of the times, a garage sale owner isn't just looking for money; they're also looking to get rid of their excess stuff. Most of the stuff that doesn't get sold is probably heading toward the trash or back to storage, so the prospect of a sale can usually convince an owner to part with the item for cheaper than he intended.

The biggest drawback to a garage sale or antique store strategy is that you are going to be buying used products, and those tend to be scrutinized by Amazon. On the off chance that you do find new products, they will most likely be in a bit of a rougher condition, which could lead some customers to complain or, worse, send it back.

Product Acquisition Strategy 6: Make it yourself

One option that you have is to create products yourself. If you are a small business owner who produces a specific product, then you can use FBA as a way to promote your product while giving it legitimacy. When someone sees a product being sold on Amazon, it gives much-needed credibility to the product. So, if you are already creating a product, you can use FBA as a way to add an additional sales venue to your company.

So, there you have it: six simple strategies that will assist you greatly in your product hunt. Now, you might be asking the question: how much should I buy? That's a great question. Your stock is important when it comes to FBA because if you end up running out of a product, you could potentially be losing sales, but at the same time, putting too much money into a product could end up costing you if it doesn't move off the shelves as quickly as you'd like. Ultimately, it is going to be a trial and error system at first. We would suggest sticking with only a few products at first and purchasing enough of them to be able to sustain a few months' worth of sales. If your stock depletes too quickly, then you know to get more for next time, but if it doesn't move, then you should know to take it easy on replenishing that specific supply.

Planning your inventory

With your newfangled FBA account, you'll probably want to start shipping items to them right away. But before you do that, it would be of value to sit down and actually figure out exactly what you want to sell. While it might be tempting to sell a hodgepodge of random things that you have laying around the house, that's not necessarily one of the best options that you have at your disposal. Instead, you should approach this as a business and come up with a strategy for *what* you are going to sell.

There are multiple approaches that an FBA seller can take; each one has different advantages and drawbacks. A sales strategy will determine what kind of inventory you are going to have. Before you commit to selling anything through FBA, you should make sure that it is on FBA's approved list. FBA has a list of approved products and will specify whether the product can be sold new or used. It's up to you to sift through that list and make sure that everything you sell is on the approved list. If it's not on the list, don't lose hope, because it just means that Amazon will need to manually approve it, which takes additional time and runs the risk of rejection.

So, here are a few different inventory strategies that an FBA seller can take.

Garage Sale Inventory:

A garage sale inventory means that you are using FBA as an opportunity to clean out your home and get rid of the junk that has been occupying your basement, your attic or your garage. Now, the biggest drawback to the garage sale inventory method is that you are most likely selling used products. There are plenty of restrictions on what can be sold used through FBA, and most customers might not be looking for a used version of the item they are browsing for. However, one of the big benefits here is that outside of the cost of shipping, you will be selling these items for pure profit since they weren't originally purchased for the purpose of sales. So, as long as you can make more money than you pay for shipping, you're in the clear! Ultimately, this kind of inventory system will only last as long as you have junk worth selling in your home. Once you run out of items that you are looking to get rid of, this sale technique's value diminishes. Still, if you're a hobbyist or just looking to make some money on the side, this is a good system.

Buy Low, Sell High:

One option that you have as a seller is to look for products that are in demand on Amazon and then look for ways to purchase them for cheap offline. Once you buy the items for cheap, you can then send them into FBA and sell them for a tidy profit. This is similar to the stock market in a sense, as the goal is to buy a product for cheap and then sell it when the value increases.

For example, you could purchase a very popular toy for some kind of discount and then during the holiday season, sell the toy online at a higher markup. Since the demand will be higher in that season, the toy will most likely be bought.

The biggest drawback to this method is that it does involve some level of risk and also requires starting capital. You must pay to acquire the item somehow, you must acquire the item for cheaper than you will sell it and most importantly, you must be able to time it right so that the market's demand will ensure that it will be sold. Still, if you do this right, you will make a larger amount of money than if you were to adopt a garage sale strategy.

Stockpile:

One option is to work on ordering products in bulk so that you can gain discounts from the sheer number that you order. Then, you send the products out online and wait for them to sell. This is less about timing the market and more about finding a product that can be purchased cheaply when ordered in large quantities and then letting it sell over time. If you're looking for a less active form of selling through FBA, this is a great method. However, the biggest drawback is that buying in bulk requires a large amount of capital upfront, and you are also going to need to spend considerable amounts of time trying to find the right supplier. Still, if you play your cards right, you could have enough of a popular product to sustain you with steady sales for months to come.

Private Label:

One option that we will be looking at in more detail in a later chapter is what's known as the Private Label. This is where you purchase a generic product and then create your own brand around it. This allows you to gain a loyal customer base who has come to prefer your brand over your competitors. In the long run, you could end up with loyal followers who purchase for a long, long time. However, this is a complicated process, and we'll go more in-depth about how to start a private label in a later chapter.

So, once you have your preferred style of inventory figured out, you must then determine exactly *what* you are going to sell. Now, at the end of the day, this is going to be more about trial and error. There are no formulas for success with FBA, so you are going to have to be willing to spend time, effort and money on products and then evaluate their performance.

You might be hesitant due to a fear of losing money on the wrong product, but try to look at it this way: whenever you lose money on a business venture, it is like you are simply paying for an education in business. Learning what doesn't work is just as vital as learning what does work, simple enough.

After you have taken some time to sit down and figure out what products you want to be shipping, you're going to need to think in the long term about how you will refresh your supply. As you make sales of your product, you will want to take some of that money, reinvest it into your product supply and maybe even expand your inventory. Let's move on to the next chapter, where we'll discuss some of the best ways to get your hands on products to sell so that you can maximize your profit.

How to Calculate Revenue

Once you have started shipping products to FBA, you should hopefully start seeing sales of your products. When you see the numbers start to increase, there can be a temptation to begin an early celebration or, worse, believe that you are making a profit.

Despite the number of sales you are making, you cannot judge your profit off of those numbers alone. Instead, you must be able to sit down, run over the books and calculate your revenue. Once you look at your revenue, you will be able to determine whether or not you are making a profit. Fortunately, you don't need a degree in accounting to calculate your revenue. Instead, Amazon actually provides a free online tool that will allow you to quickly calculate the revenue on each product.

    This tool can be found at Amazon Seller Central and is available for no additional cost, so feel free to use it as much as you want. You should be in the habit of regularly checking revenue streams for each product that you have available to ensure that it remains profitable. Don't make the mistake of thinking that sales equal profit. Sales can easily be eaten up by the cost of shipping, storage costs, returns, etc.

The revenue calculator will ask for a significant amount of information, and this is information that you must make sure to keep track of. Never round up, eyeball it or just guess, because when you have inaccurate data, you will get inaccurate results. You must have a laser-like focus when it comes to recording the financial data because money is the lifeblood of your organization. If you aren't treating this like a day job, then it could be tempting to be lazy, but regardless of your commitment level, you need to be respectful of your money. Only people who respect their money will gain more of it in the future.

So, this means that you should have some method of tracking your expenses and costs. The revenue calculator is only as handy as the data that you input, so try to keep that in mind. One simple way to keep track of all of your money expenditures is to use a simple program, like QuickBooks, or if you don't want to spend the extra cash, use a spreadsheet.

What do you need to be tracking? Pretty much anything that involves your money. If you spend money, then you should mark where, when and how much you have spent. Keep separate logs for each product that you are selling online and record the shipping costs as well as the fees for using the Amazon Fulfillment Centers. Once you have all of these numbers logged, you can then use the reports from Amazon to input data into the revenue calculator.

This is a crucial step, and it cannot be overlooked if you want to make good money. A lot of times, you will hear Amazon success stories from people who are just reporting the sales and not the actual net profit. These folks might be convinced that they are making a fortune online, but once you look at the numbers and see that they are paying more money than they are bringing in, you can know their efforts are in vain.

There is a second benefit to keeping a tight track of the revenue stream that you have developed: efficiency. Once you have the ability to glance at a product's performance and determine whether it is profitable or not, you can choose to invest more money in the product, lower prices, eliminate it from your stock entirely or advertise more for it. Sales are not just indications of you getting richer, but rather they are extremely valuable pieces of data.

Sales have the ability to communicate market demands to you. They essentially allow you to determine your business strategy. Everything is a theory until the sales begin to show you what the market is interested in. Products that fly off the shelf should be restocked quickly, products that sit around and never move should be phased out. No amount of research, studying and science can accurately aid you in building a strategy more than pure, raw numbers. These are the only things that don't lie in business. By learning to pay attention to the numbers, you will learn how to continue to develop your strategy.

As you can see, there is a tremendous reward in calculating revenues and keeping a close eye on your product sales. Of course, we should note that the FBA business is a long game, so products don't necessarily need to turn around quickly, but if you're going more than a few months without a single sale, chances are there are some things that you could be doing differently.

Chapter 15: Affiliate Marketing and Other Income Streams

Your next best bet is affiliate marketing. Before we get into the potential, let's just look at what that is for those of you who are not in the field. Affiliate marketing is the business of marketing goods and services that you do not produce, design or manufacture. You do not even take stock of the product, or put up cash to purchase inventory whilst you make a sale. All it entails is the need to market goods that others manufacture and have for sale. A person who clicks on an advertisement or a link that you are hosting is a potential customer. If he or she makes the purchase after clicking on the link that was on your site, a portion of the revenue from that sale is then paid to you.

You should be starting to see the potential here. There are many ways you can take advantage of this opportunity. The key to this is that the name of the game is traffic. Traffic comes from visitors, who can either be your social followers or someone finding yours from search engine results, so what you are looking at is search engine optimization (SEO).

Nathan Michaud
Outsourcing to Make Passive Income

The secret that you need to know is that any business can be advanced to a point that it earns revenue and profit on autopilot. As long as you can outsource everything cost-effectively and reliably, then you can make any business, even a lemonade stand, into something that generates passive income. The passive income model is highly prevalent and suited to most online businesses.

A few things you need to know is that you have to find a reliable source of talent. Whether it is non-fiction writers for your self-publishing business or copywriters to compose compelling sales letters, voice talent to record jingles and audiobooks, or graphic designers to make YouTube intros and outros, you need a source out to sites like freelancer.com or guru.com to find the right talent.

Once you hire that person, the relationship is not chiseled in stone. This is not the conventional hiring and obligation kind of endeavor. It results in a variable cost model where you are not forced to pay a fixed salary in months when business is slow.

Hiring freelancers and outsourcing your needs to outsiders allows you to get the best talent for the job at hand. You can then get a virtual assistant to manage the entire process. The key success factor in creating passive income is that you have a clear understanding of the process and each person you hire must be given a strong set of instructions and procedures to follow so that there is no misunderstanding and wasted effort and time.

The assets that you have in this case are related to any kind of content that someone would search for, or someone would repeatedly come back to you for. One way is to have a loyal following on YouTube, Twitter or Facebook. These social media followers are pliable and can easily be persuaded to click on links.

You can break the entire process down into content, clicks, and cash – the 3C's of affiliate marketing. This can also be done in such a way that you automate much of the process, and that will allow a large part of your work to be front-loaded and, after you get the system right, you just have to sit back and let it take on a life of its own. As long as you have someone constantly supplying content, and keep growing your social media following, then you will be able to keep the traffic constantly circulating through your website assets and that will bring about clicks on your links. Once set up, they practically run by themselves and do especially well if you get a virtual assistant to watch over things.

To be able to do this successfully, there are a few different avenues that you can follow to get clicks. Among all the business that you could possibly do, affiliate marketing can even be done on a smaller scale where you focus on the content that you are really a master of. So, let's say that you are really good at knitting. If you have a website and blog where you provide knitting advice and how-to's, and you get people to follow your blog and read your content, then you could get products that relate to knitting and have links to places like Amazon. This means that if your reader likes your article and wants to follow along, they just follow your link and, when they make the purchase, voila! You get a piece of the action. This is a credible source of passive income while you go about doing something related to your main business or interest. It's a way of monetizing your professional content, or the monetizing of your interests.

The brilliance of affiliate marketing is that it can run as a standalone, or it can be something that you do in parallel to a related or unrelated business. Its flexibility affords you multiple paths to success, and it is only limited by your imagination. The web is filled with resources and you can make this as small or as big as you want.

Youtube Marketing For Dropshipping

Everyone loves YouTube videos. Most news and current affairs that people consume come exclusively from the YouTube platform, and then there are hobby-related videos and special interest content and even job improvement skills also on YouTube.

There are some occasions that the YouTube content and format don't suit what you may be looking for but, for the most part, the content that is presented will provide you with what you are looking for. That's the beauty of Google - you get exactly what you want, or you just end the video and find something else.

The point is that YouTube videos are highly informative, entertaining and are especially relevant when looking for product reviews, how-to videos and movie previews.

So, the question comes down to how do you make YouTube something that will earn you passive income? The idea behind passive income is to put in a bit of work upfront, and for that work to result in a product that continuously generates traffic by those looking for the kind of content that you have uploaded.

In terms of YouTube, once uploaded and it is of interest, viewership is almost automatic. What you get from it is a share of revenue from the viewership. On average, YouTube publishers make about $1,000 per million views from one video. There is no limit to how many videos a publisher can place. When you first start out, you may only be allowed to put in videos that are short – less than 20 minutes. After some time, they will remove those limitations and you will be able to publish those longer videos.

There are two things that you have to know. The first is that, for those of you who are just starting off, there are numerous types of video editing software that is free. If you have an Apple computer, then there are some really powerful apps that will create videos and sound and give you powerful editing and cutting features. The videos that you make from these are of good quality, and you will be able to publicize your business in interesting ways.

There is one channel where a private jet pilot, who spends his days ferrying people in his jet, records the whole flight. The video channel has good audio and video quality, and he uses the GoPro camera mounted in multiple locations in the cockpit. Videos usually last for about an hour as he goes about flying his airplane. He has never, even once, had to adjust the cameras. He then uploads them once he has landed. The videos attract about 50,000 views per video.

This is the epitome of passive income. Passive income doesn't just mean that you publish something and off you go to the beaches for your Mai Tai. It also means that you can earn a little extra while your main business is in the foreground. There is a carpenter out in Colorado that has something similar to the private pilot that was mentioned earlier.

The carpenter channel has about 40,000 views per video

and the two of them (the carpenter and the pilot) have a differing frequency of video production. The brilliant thing about it is that you can make it so that each time they publish a video, you get a notification. From the point of publishing, these guys get to their target viewership numbers within a few days of uploading the video.

These may be small potatoes, but, for passive income, it's hard to beat. The top YouTube producer made over $12,000,000 in 2017. That was not passive income in entirety because there is a lot of promotion that goes into the more recent videos but, with good quality and good content, the revenue adds up. The top ten earners make more than $100,000,000 in ad-related revenue. Not bad for sitting in front of a computer.

Selling Info Products

There is a huge confusion on what info products really are. Info products are exactly what you think; except maybe look at it from this way – what are physical products? Physical products are things that have a physical form. In the same way, info products are products that are informational and usually things that you can download. They don't include music and entertainment products, but, rather, they include books, instructions, reviews, and even courses.

In the other parts of this book, we talked (and will talk) about books, audiobooks, and videos. That means it's best if we leave info products as the products that relate to information that people are looking for in terms of e-books, and downloadable content that provides information of value, like courses.

If you have not heard about this, there are sites like Udemy.com where anyone wanting to learn something can look for a course and purchase it. They will get e-books, videos, and documents that will give them an idea into the topic they are looking for. So, let's say that you are a really good photographer, and what you do is create a course in photography and offer it on Udemy. People will buy it and your course stays there for however long you want it to. You are then able to collect passive income from it over the next few years, especially if your course is popular. In 2017, the top course provider earned close to $3 million. If you are a college professor, a flight instructor, or a diving instructor, you can make a course while you are actually teaching your students and make that into a course that you place on Udemy. That will result in passive income that is spun off your main job; passive income that parallels your full-time job. You can't beat that.

If you want to take it one step further, then what you can do is hire teachers to make courses, pay them a fair amount and they convert that into a course, together with e-books and apps. In this way, you can have any course and have any number of them. The profit potential for these videos of info products are especially for their passive income potential. In most businesses, you do the job once, and you get paid once. If you want to get more income, you have to do it all over again. With passive income strategies like the ones mentioned in this book, you just have to do it once and, after a while, you get passive income from across your offerings – with no expiration attached to it.

Print on Demand Merch

For those of you who are not writers or editors, or inclined to deal with the stresses of self-publishing, then there is another way that you could get on the online entrepreneurial bandwagon, and that is to start designing t-shirts.

Before you start thinking about sourcing the material and getting a seamstress or a factory to produce the t-shirt, stop right there. You don't need to do any of that. T-shirt design is not about sewing and printing, it's about designing, and Amazon has a new service where you print on demand. Well, actually, you give it to them, and they will print it whenever an order comes in.

So, here is how it works: You design what goes on the t-shirt and send Amazon the artwork. There is an online page that you can upload it to. You will decide the price, Amazon will tell you the cost, and they will take a cut from the sale.

You make money each time someone purchases your design. The buyer will sort out what size they want, and Amazon will do the printing and the shipping. You can just spend your day doodling and designing what goes on the t-shirt.

Their service is called Merch by Amazon and you can tie it to your existing Amazon accounts. Be warned though, as, at the moment, Merch is by invitation only, so if you want to be invited, just send them a request and they will ask to see some of your prior designs and then you should get accepted.

Once you get in, here is how you make money with it. You can't just leave it there and hope that someone buys it. That's too passive, even for passive income. You need to tie it to some kind of product, brand, or event. If you have a product that you are selling elsewhere, you can brand that product, like games, or you can even have them made as part of a club or group and then direct your buyers to make the purchase on Amazon. Just send them a link.

Here is another trick to make a few extra bucks from each sale. Get an affiliate account with Amazon so that, when you send your customers a link to buy the t-shirt on Merch, all you have to do is send that affiliate link and, not only will you get the income from Amazon, but you will also get an additional affiliate income from them as well. Don't worry, it's not double dipping and Amazon doesn't mind when you do that. Most people do.

T-shirts are a huge business and something that most people need and buy repeatedly. You can do them in vivid color, or you can do them in classic black and white or monochrome.

What if you have no idea how to design, and have no insight into the designing process? Well, there is a way out from that too. Freelancer.com has a feature where you can advertise for a contest and have designers design for you and then you chose the one that you like. Once you have that design, pay the designer then transfer that to your Merch account and get the t-shirts with that design.

There is another way to make money with this by cross-selling the t-shirts with your books and audiobooks. You can sell them on your info products, or you can sell them on the YouTube videos that you produce. The possibilities are endless. What you need to do is just make the decision to do it.

Chapter 16: Outsourcing For Dropshipping

The biggest part of taking full advantage of a laptop lifestyle is to be part of a collaborative community. The guy on the other end of the instant messaging system that is doing your work for you is also making money on a laptop. The difference is that his business is task-based and has no room for passive income. Yours does, so make use of it as this is your lucky day.

The key to this is finding good people and find back-ups to those people so that you can keep the production cycle going. There are apps and software that you can purchase rather inexpensively that will give you an idea of what are the best titles that are being sold, and the ones that are popular. From there, you can cross-reference that with the keywords that prospective buyers are searching for and, from there, you can come up on the titles that will most likely be successful.

Once you have your titles, go to a site like freelancer.com and look for writers who can produce manuscripts that will satisfy the keywords. Your best spot to find all the freelancers you need is to use freelancer.com and you will find that payments are easy and you can get writers, editors, and voice over artists with a convenient one-stop payment potential. In essence, you can treat freelancer.com as your HR department.

Once you have that sorted out, create a manual or a booklet on the various operating procedures. List all the steps that are necessary to produce the audiobook. Keep track of all the steps that work, and make it as efficient as possible, Set a goal for how many audiobooks you want to create, and then go out and get it done.

In all this, the key success factor to making millions in the first year is to make sure that you have strong content. The quality of your content must be one that keeps the readers coming back for more.

The second area that you need to develop is a follower base. You can do this through subscriptions to your blog, or with social media followers. If you have to, pay someone who is an expert to build a social media presence, and pay someone to do search engine optimization. Neither is expensive.

For now, let's concentrate on content development.

Content development covers a wide area. Anything that you can write about and anything that a consumer consumes that is intangible can be considered content. E-books, audiobooks, music, data, knowledge products, games, apps, and software are all kinds of content, and most of the time they are downloadable without the need to go to the store and physically pick it up.

You need to master the content development cycle and then take that and feed it into the marketing and conversion cycle. The content development cycle begins with understanding what niche would sell well, or give you a good return. If you can understand what the returns are, you can determine what level of costs you are willing to be subjected to.

In drop shipping, you have to have a certain amount of cash on hand, or at least credit, to be able to make the purchases from your vendor, but this is significantly less in amount compared to purchasing the inventory before you sell it to your customer. Drop shipping allows you to only purchase from your vendor once a customer purchased from you. To do this well, you need to have a constant track of your suppliers' inventory and stock levels.

You can even combine drop shipping with online storefronts as well as on Amazon. It is a little different from FBA in the sense that you do not need to make a huge purchase then ship it to an Amazon warehouse; now, you just sell on Amazon's regular marketplace but have it sent directly from the seller.

There are benefits and drawbacks to both. When most online entrepreneurs start they do one business at a time. There is a learning curve, but it is by no means a steep curve. To help do the homework, read the material and get yourself up to speed. Once you get a little familiar with this, you can then get content out and promote it in a number of ways. Focus on this area first, and then, as the processes start to work, you can start to outsource most of it and then you will be able to move to the next facet of your laptop lifestyle. That brings us to the next chapter on outsourcing.

Conclusion

Now, all that you need to do is get started immediately. In the words of the wise Master Oogway from Kung-Fu Panda, "Today is a gift and that's why it's known as the present." So, there is no time like the present to get started. The idea of starting a business on your own can be a little daunting. You need to gather your courage and take the first step. If you put in the necessary hard work, dedicate your time and be a little patient, you can become the owner of a successful business.

It is quite unfortunate that a lot of businesses tend to fail in their first year. If you don't want to be amongst them, then you need the necessary motivation and determination to succeed. Failure is part and parcel of life. Learn from the mistakes you face, and you can overcome any hurdle that comes your way. It is not easy to succeed, have no qualms about it, but once you do, there is nothing that can replicate the high of success.

Made in the USA
Middletown, DE
12 March 2019